Stuff I Wish I Knew Earlier

Stuff I Wish I Knew Earlier

How to Unlock Your Career Potential

Soon-to-Be-Grad Edition

Luki Danukarjanto

IGUANA

Copyright © 2017 Luki Danukarjanto

Published by Iguana Books
720 Bathurst Street, Suite 303
Toronto, Ontario, Canada
M5S 2R4

All rights reserved. No part of this publication may be reproduced, stored in a retrieval system or transmitted, in any form or by any means, electronic, mechanical, recording or otherwise (except brief passages for purposes of review) without the prior permission of the author or a licence from The Canadian Copyright Licensing Agency (Access Copyright). For an Access Copyright licence, visit www.accesscopyright.ca or call toll free to 1-800-893-5777.

Publisher: Mary Ann J. Blair
Editor: Jen R. Albert
Front cover image: Jessica Albert
Author photograph: Ariana Kris Photography http://www.arianakris.com

ISBN (paperback): 978-1-77180-239-0
ISBN (hardcover): 978-1-77180-242-0
ISBN (EPUB): 978-1-77180-240-6
ISBN (Kindle): 978-1-77180-241-3

This is an original print edition of *Stuff I Wish I Knew Earlier*.

To all the people who are lost or stuck in their careers, this is for you. But also for my wife, kids, and family in helping me reach my potential.

Contents

Acknowledgements xi

Luki's Disclaimer xiii

Introduction 1
   The origin story 1
   SIWIKE: Stuff I Wish I Knew Earlier 4
   Only for soon-to-be-grads? 4
   Guiding principles 5

Part One: Vision 7
   Chapter 1: A Grand Adventure of Your Own Design 9
      Prioritizing yourself and your future 9
      It's your choice, so seek success 11
      Career success starts with school success 16
      Post-secondary education isn't for everyone — and that's okay ... 19
      Evaluate what success means to you 21
   Chapter 2: Who Are You and What Do You Want? 25
      Are you a chef or cook? 25
      Self-awareness is everything 27
      Know your own tendencies 30
      Focus on your strengths; make your weaknesses irrelevant ... 31
      Your value lies in your passions 37
      Find your *why* before figuring out your *how* 39
      Your purpose may be the source of your brand 42

Chapter 3: Summary — Vision 44
    Vision: Resources 44

Part 2: Preparation 51
    Chapter 4: Check Your Vitals 53
        A little self-care goes a long way 53
        Take pride in your personal presentation 55
        There's power in the present moment 56
        Emotions have intelligence 59
        Cultivate your confidence 60
        Have a growth mindset 63
        All learning starts with memory 65
    Chapter 5: You're More Wealthy Than You Think 73
        Create an abundance mindset 73
        Good money management is learned, not inherited 75
        Credit or convenience 80
        Profit from the side hustle 81
    Chapter 6: Communication Is Connection 84
        Relationships matter as much as results 86
        Adapt your communication style 94
        It's better to be understood than heard 97
        Don't just be interesting; be interested 98
    Chapter 7: Summary — Preparation 100
        Preparation: Resources 100

Part 3: Skill Building 103
    Chapter 8: Motivation and Productivity Hacks 105
        Motivation fuels your success; procrastination is the enemy 105
        Your results are determined by your expectations 106
        You are in control of your habits 107
        Time management is attention management 114

Chapter 9: Job Hunt 123
    Everyone is a salesperson 125
    In every role, there is a "customer" to be served 126
    Reverse-engineer the job you want.. 126
    Focus on accomplishments, not activities, on your resume 127
    Practice your interview skills.. 128
    Hiring is seasonal — know when to apply 131
    Work experience is the shortcut to going pro 131
    Your job hunt never ends... 132
    Gain experience managing up, beside, and below 133
    Essential tips and tools for job seekers 137

Chapter 10: The New Networking... 146
    Introverts can network, too 146
    Networking does not have to be sleazy — Build Meaningful Connections 149
    Networking is not a crapshoot 150
    It pays to be the dumbest person in the room 153
    Future opportunities come from past connections 154

Chapter 11: Summary — Skill Building.. 157
    Skill building: Resources 158

Part 4: Expansion 161

Chapter 12: Lifelong Learning 163
    Your first job is not forever 163
    The path to success is rarely straight or narrow....................... 163
    Add to and adjust your career bucket list.................................. 165
    Find your inner critic 168
    Knowledge shared is knowledge multiplied............................. 170
    You've got more time than you think.. 171
    All my dreams can come true — but not all at once................. 172

    You can create your passion 174
Chapter 13: Unstoppable 176
    Live life in the front row.. 176
    Mediocrity is the enemy 177
    Seek mastery... 178
    You can run your own company.. 180
    There's no time like the present 181
Chapter 14: Summary — Expansion 182
Chapter 15: Where Will Your Awesomeness Take You? 183
Commemoration 187

Acknowledgements

Thank you for taking the time to read this book. You could have been doing something else, yet you chose to read my content. I hope that you can turn this knowledge into results.

I want to thank my wife, Clara, for supporting me throughout my transition and the growth that has come since. I love you. To my two sons, Keane and Lochlan, it will be interesting to see what they become given all the SIWIKE they'll be getting.

Thank you to my parents, who gave me all the support a son could ask for, and to my sisters and brother, who each had a hand in teaching me while we continue to grow up together, and who were all subjected to the early version of this book before we passed the first editing hurdle (sorry for that and hopefully this version makes up for it).

Many thanks to the GNO boys: my high school friends who still support me. To all my mentors and colleagues from Deloitte with special recognition to John Mavriyannakis, Stephen Resar, Ravi Mohabir, Cielito Ward, D'Arcy Mathias, Jeff Bowman, Karl Lui, Kelvin Kang, and Paul Held. Whether you knew it or not, I learned a ton from you. I would love to single out everyone else, but this would be the consulting address book of Canada if I were to list everyone. To everyone who has formally and informally mentored me, I truly appreciate you and this SIWIKE's for you.

Thanks to the (official and unofficial) team that helped evolve FOCUS Inspired: Bonnie Wong, Stan Ly, Eva Yung, Garros Fung, Ben Wan, Karee Chen, and Josephine Ahady, who continue to be great champions of the FOCUS Inspired mission to unlock the career potential of everyone. They are constant (or just occasional) sounding boards for my crazy ideas, and they provide sanity checks to keep me focused and grounded.

Thanks to Jen Albert for doing a fantastic editing job and making my writing more readable. As well as Kelvin Kong, Mary Ann Blair, Greg Ioannou, Maggie Langrick, Michelle MacAleese, and Scott Fraser, who helped with various stages of the publication of the book. Thanks to my initial version proofreaders: Jason Yeung and Youyee Chen. To Martin Buktaw for cover art concepts and Jessica Albert for the cover art design. Plus all the friends who voted for their favourite cover design.

Thanks to all my clients who let me help them. I'll be a little corny and say that you've probably helped me more than I helped you.

And finally, to my mentors I have yet to meet, I hope I have done justice in DJing out your messages. I plan to personally shake your hand one day to thank you for the insights you've provided.

Luki's Disclaimer

I call myself a DJ for personal and professional development. A DJ (or disc jockey) mixes different sources of recorded music, sometimes adding their own beats to produce a different experience. I mix what I've learned from others with my own experiences and play it back. Many popular beats are just a repackaging of music from generations before. The same thing can be applied to advice about personal and professional development. Many of these concepts have been popularized in recent years, but some have actually been around for decades, centuries, and sometimes millennia. Did Christopher Columbus create the Americas? Perhaps. He definitely made it known to a part of the world that was previously unaware of its existence. Similarly, I give credit to those from whom I have learned. The material they've produced echoes what I understand. I have by no means consumed all the content out there, and if something is not attributed, it does not mean that I created it. It just means that I haven't yet encountered a specific resource that details the content, and I am looking to popularize it for the benefit of the readers.

As you read the content of the book, don't do anything because I say so. Do it because you agree with it and feel it would add value to you. Dive into the content in more detail just as you might listen to the original track in the DJ's mix. And consult a professional if you're really stuck!

With that said, let's get on with the show!

Introduction

You have amazing potential. You know it. In your heart. In your soul. The feeling might be exceptionally strong, or a little more subdued. But you know you have the potential for greatness.

You might know exactly what that potential is, but not how to use or unlock it. Or you might not know what it is, but you feel you can give the world much more than you're on track for now. But how…

Don't worry. I was exactly the same as you. And I've helped many like us to get on a path to reach their career potential. I hope that you are excited to join me as I recount my journey from moderate achievement to success, as I know you will see parallels to your own journey.

Before I share the guidance that will get you on the path to unlocking your potential, I should tell you a bit about myself, shouldn't I?

The origin story

I was born in Jakarta, Indonesia, and my parents decided to move to Canada when I was about three years old. I had a typical middle-class upbringing. (Nothing to make a movie about.) I grew up and decided on a degree in computer science for a few reasons: my dad worked at IBM, the dot-com bubble was growing (so everything was about Silicon Valley this and Silicon Valley that), and I was a teenage boy who liked video games. My university life wasn't anything special. Oh, I almost failed out of my co-op program in first year. Sorry, Mom and Dad, if you're reading this for the first time, but hey, I made it through. Eventually I settled in and started doing reasonably well. Enough to pass at least. But not enough to make the dean's list and achieve what most parents want for their kids.

And great timing on my part, as I graduated just as the dot-com bubble burst. Luckily, I had some work experience through the co-op program. So I was getting interviews and job offers here and there. Luckier still, I had a friend whose brother was looking for a coder. He helped me get an interview, and I ended up getting the job (actually, I jumped for joy after the recruiter hung up the phone, so it was a big deal). The job was as a coder, and perhaps luckiest, it was with Deloitte as part of their technology consulting service area. And it started out great! Unfortunately, I realized a few short months later that I didn't like coding. I had thought I didn't like coding in school because it was school. So, it was tough to say to myself that maybe I didn't make the right decision. Crap! I was stuck. Or was I?

Fortunately, my luck continued as there was a team on the other side of the floor that always seemed to be having fun. I asked them what they did. "Sourcing and procurement," they said. I had no idea what that was but asked if they needed any help. "Sure, we need a technical lead," was the answer. I figured that a technical lead just manages a bunch of coders, and I thought to myself, *Hey, I can manage a whole bunch of me*. And a few conversations later, I was in.

Here's where it starts getting a little more exciting. After that technical lead role, I was catapulted into a flurry of other roles that helped me explore different career opportunities. They needed a functional lead. When I had sat in workshops as a technical lead, I'd seen the functional person drawing boxes and arrows to design the business process and thought, *I could do that*. They needed a testing lead. Well, if I had designed the system, I should be able to figure out how to test that it works. They needed a training lead. If I had designed and tested the system, you would hope I could teach you how to use it. And if I had basically done all of that, I might as well run the whole project. Then if I've run these projects, I could advise other companies on the risk and challenges for future ones. And so on, until twelve years later, I was leading my own practice area consisting of twenty to twenty-five people, working on several million-dollar projects. The next step in my career would have been becoming a partner — basically a C-level executive position. Not bad for someone who thought they were stuck a few paragraphs earlier.

What might be more interesting is, while I helped build the practice area, I was given the opportunity to help Deloitte's undergrad campus recruiting team. I started coordinating between our business partners, our human resource (HR) team, and the schools. Then I began working with the HR team to organize events, and manage the candidate screening process. Then we started growing the team based on our increasing hiring targets. We added a few initiatives here and there, all while continuing to be a consultant by day. Eventually, I oversaw the undergrad hiring process from end to end. That also meant I owned the list of hires across all universities in Canada before it was sent to the partners for final hiring approval.

From most accounts, I was in an enviable position. It came to a pause, when I had what I call my "quarter-career crisis." No need to cry for me, as the "crisis" was in the first-world-problem sense where I was in a good job but thought that I was meant to do something else. The crisis wasn't new, and it hit its tipping point while I was travelling for a project. I was FaceTiming with my wife and found out that my son had learned to roll over. I realized that he had had many firsts that I only heard about after the fact. And we had a second child coming.

The crisis came from knowing a decision had to be made: continue on a lucrative career path in a prestigious firm *or* be with my family. I spent a lot of time soul-searching, speaking to mentors, consuming content, and self-reflecting. Through that process, there was a spark: to help others find the purpose. It ignited into a passion. I found my purpose to help others find their purpose. To the firm's credit, I was given a lot of support and options to stay. I had an interest in helping people, so we thought perhaps I should move into the human capital consulting group. Or support people development internally. I was even offered the chance to create my own role to add value to the firm. But I realized I had always wanted to start something on my own. With childhood dreams of opening a restaurant, a tutoring school, and other endeavours, the passion kept burning and it got too challenging to put out. So, I made the hard decision to leave a prestigious job to start my own career-coaching venture. I prepared myself for the potential ridicule of leaving a very promising career to starting up something and scraping by for the next little while. But, when I reconnected with people to tell them of my departure, and I explained my career-coaching future, I was pleasantly surprised that many of them thought it made sense. They had always seen me as a coach and wished me well as they knew I could help a lot of people. Maybe that meant I was on the right track.

Fast-forward to today: I catalyze many young professionals on a path to career success and I have a positive impact on people's lives. I hope one of them will be yours. Allow me to share my SIWIKE®.

SIWIKE: Stuff I Wish I Knew Earlier

Before I made my decision to leave the firm, I went through a journey of self-reflection. I needed to justify to myself that it was the right decision. I looked back to find pivotal times in my career. These were times where I was enlightened by a truth, which had I known ten, five, or even one year earlier, would have completely altered my career trajectory, likely in the upward direction. At this time, I started absorbing as much information as I could through books, podcasts, and YouTube videos. I read more during that period than I had in the three decades before combined. As I consumed the content, I often found myself occasionally nodding along with the material when I found a tactic or concept aligned with one of my enlightened moments. This was the stuff I wish I knew earlier. Then it dawned on me. Someone knew about that information way before I did. Some of the content was written decades, if not centuries, before. If that was the case, how many others didn't know the information? And wouldn't someone benefit from knowing the Stuff I Wish I Knew Earlier? That's how I discovered SIWIKE.

> SIWIKE originally started as "The stuff you did not know you needed to know." Try that on for an acronym. It morphed into I Wish I Knew That Earlier, then changed to SYWYKE (Stuff You Wish You Knew Earlier) then I realized I shouldn't be so presumptuous and changed it to *I*. I settled on SIWIKE.

Only for soon-to-be-grads?

While you might think that a soon-to-be-grad is someone in their last year of university, the ideal scenario is that you would have found this book in your first year, or perhaps even in high school. Many of the rewards gained from executing the SIWIKE in the book are immediate, while others take time to incubate. For those rewards, the longer you have, the better.

If you only found out about the book after graduation, the content would still be useful, as you can apply the information starting now even if you didn't have the luxury of doing so in school.

Guiding principles

You have probably been given a lot of direction thus far. I don't want to add more constraints; however, these guiding principles should help you as you consume and apply the information in this book to make it your own.

Here are two guiding principles for the book:

1. Be you: In this book, I share my experiences and SIWIKE as well as those of others. Take this information and learn from it. But not so that you can be more like us. Instead, figure out what parts apply to you and learn how to be more like you. Treat the content of this book like the offerings at a buffet restaurant. Pile your plate high and try a bit of everything. Then go back and get seconds and thirds of what resonates with you. Take the opportunity to discover yourself as well.

2. Go to the source: I distill, paraphrase, and share my perspectives on the SIWIKE that has come from others. I have compiled the content shared here, making it more concise using my personal perspective filters. You might find a different meaning or have a different interpretation of or application for the original content. For added insight and ideas, take the time to find and learn from the original resources I mention.

Part One: Vision

In my culture, there are several preferred career paths. Becoming a doctor, lawyer, engineer, or accountant is preferred. Every other career path is somehow considered second-rate. Although I was influenced by that unspoken sentiment, I am thankful that my parents let me choose what path I wanted to pursue as a career.

In hindsight, I wasn't the type to go against the societal norm anyways. A degree in computer science wasn't a preferred career path, but since computer science was engineering's close cousin, and the dot-com bubble hadn't yet burst, a career in computers was acceptable. And to be honest, in my circles, science, technology, engineering, and math (STEM) was king, so a degree in business or humanities would have made me a second-class citizen. Or at least that was my impression. If you went into the social sciences, you were just settling. Does any of that sound familiar to you?

Maybe not, but I've encountered many people for whom the sentiment was the same, but the categories were different. With one, business was number one. With another, if you ended up in anything but social sciences then you hadn't really found your passion and were just taking a degree to make your parents happy. Or perhaps those expectations were just self-imposed to hold themselves back from unlocking their potential.

What I've realized, and hope you can too, is that others' expectations do not really matter. The most important vision for your future is your own. That vision might not be easy to know. I can sympathize that you have various circumstances beyond your control. An economic situation that doesn't allow you the same flexibility and opportunities that other people have. Strict or traditional parents who place the expectations they had for themselves on you. Or other conditions that seem to cause you to struggle more than others. Whatever situation you are in, it is hard. And what are you planning to do about it? As you think about your challenges and complaints, reflect on that question. You can choose to accept it. Or you can choose to do something about it. One of the most significant SIWIKE I've come across: It's your choice.

Chapter 1: A Grand Adventure of Your Own Design

When I used to think about my future, my vision of what I was going to do was quite standard:

1. Go to school for something I liked doing.
2. Get a well-paying job in my field.
3. Settle down — get married, live in that two-car garage home in the suburbs with two kids and a dog (or cat if my wife ended up liking cats more, since I wasn't really a pet person).

As I mentioned in my origin story, the first step didn't quite happen as expected, which in hindsight was quite fortunate. Otherwise, I might not have ended up being a leader in a management consulting company, finding an interest and passion in people development, or starting my own company, let alone writing a book. The plans for the future have me building an interactive app based on the principles of this book and opening a school for soft skills to help transform education. I tell you this not to brag, but to help you understand that I too had humble beginnings, and that you can achieve all that you strive for and more than you thought possible. How? Start by taking a look at your priorities.

Prioritizing yourself and your future

You've likely heard about compound interest. Start saving early and your money will grow more than if you start later. For example, if you were to invest $20,000 between the ages of twenty and thirty and let it grow at a modest 6% interest rate until you retired at sixty and your friend also saved $20,000 at the same 6% rate between the ages of thirty and forty, you would have more than triple the savings compared to your late-investing friend! Starting early pays.

Why does compound interest belong in a section about prioritizing yourself? Prioritizing yourself is compound interest for your life; investments in your personal and professional development compound just like they do for money.

Whether you're in school or working or doing something else, investing in yourself is a good idea. Why? It's the one investment that no one can take away from you. If you invest in the stock market, the market can crash and wipe out your portfolio. If you invest in real estate, a natural disaster or other calamity could decimate your assets. At the end of the day (barring any catastrophic personal mental or physical tragedy), you'll always have what's in between your ears as skills and experience to help you take on your next opportunity!

TRY THIS: Add non-negotiable time as an investment in yourself

I suggest people create "non-negotiable time" (NN-time), time during the week when you can focus on any personal and professional development. It's non-negotiable because if a friend asks you to come out during this time, you must say no. Favourite show or movie will be airing on TV? You can't! You need to work on yourself. Hungry and want to get a snack? Think again! You're on the road to being a better you. Need to go to the bathroom? Nope! Well maybe not that sadistic, but you could have easily gone before you started, so that just points to the fact that you need to learn to manage your time. How much NN-time, you ask?

I suggest starting with a one-hour block. Pick a day of the week and be consistent. Let's say Sunday 8–9 p.m., or whatever works within your schedule. You should be able to find at least one hour a week. Then add a half-hour on a different day. Then another day. Or increase it to one and a half or two or more hours until you have set aside several hours for NN-time every week.

Spend that time doing something related to personal or professional development. Consider doing one or more of the following:

- Do research.
- Read.
- Update your resume or LinkedIn page.
- Message people to build your relationships.
- Reflect on the week.
- Contribute to one of your other SIWIKE goals.

Here are a few rules of NN-time:

1. Be consistent about the day and time of NN-time.
2. You can pre-execute your NN-time, but you cannot defer it. If a once-in-a-lifetime event happens during this time and you decide to negotiate with yourself, you must negotiate forward and not backward. For example, if your NN-time is Sunday at 8–10 p.m., you could do it earlier on Sunday or on Saturday, or earlier in the week. But you cannot do it later.
3. The activities you do during NN-time should not have a due date. That means, NN-time is *not* extra time during the week to catch up on assignments.
4. NN-time is time when you are investing in improving yourself. This means it is *not* time to unwind as you click on endless YouTube videos or Snapchat stories.
5. If you're sending messages to connect with people, you can send out as many messages you want, but during your NN-time, you cannot respond to any messages. Sending out messages is proactive. Responding to them is reactive.

Regardless of how you decide to structure your NN-time, making the time for yourself is one of the most important SIWIKE I've found in unlocking career potential.

Up next...

You've set up NN-time in your life and prioritized yourself. You just need to avoid the habit of negotiating with yourself. Those investments in yourself might not seem like much now, but trust me, they will pay dividends later.

You're a priority. The next step will be to make your choices.

It's your choice, so seek success

Think about the last time you and your friends had to pick a place for dinner. How long does that choice take? I know some of my groups of friends need to go through several rounds of, "I don't know, what do *you* want?" But let's say you're quick and the group is small, so it only takes five minutes to decide. Dinner takes about two hours (or 120 minutes), so for even a simple activity like dinner, it takes you 4 percent of the time to choose dinner versus the length of the dinner.

Now, why did I start this section with a scenario about choosing a place to eat? You would probably agree that picking your career is much more important than choosing a place for dinner, but most people spend more time deciding where to have dinner than what to do for their career. Let me explain. A working career is roughly 80,000 hours.[1] If we take 4 percent of that number, that amounts to over a year and a half. How long did you really spend on choosing your future career? Be honest. If I were honest with myself, I'd admit that I probably spent a few days thinking about the different universities and programs I wanted to apply to. More time was probably spent filling in the applications than making the decisions. So, if I added up all the time I spent, together it might have added up to a week.

One difference between where you go to school and your future career is that your choice of university or educational program does not permanently select your career path. So why not spend some of your time at school to validate your choice? That time could be during the summer between high school and university or during your studies throughout the school year. Suppose you decide to take a degree in accounting. Or sociology or engineering or biology or whatever. Is that a good choice for you? Perhaps, and wouldn't it be good to get hands-on experience to understand what choice you really made? That is of course assuming that you are the one making the choice to follow that direction.

Following your North Star versus Steering the Ship

The North Star is an analogy for your career journey. In the old seafaring days, well before the time of GPS, ships navigated at night using the constellations. People noticed that the stars followed specific patterns, and if you followed them repeatedly, you'd tend to end up in the same approximate area. As you got closer, you'd be able to see your destination and make the necessary course corrections to get there.

You can see how the analogy relates to your career direction. Your degree and future career is your North Star. The direction you're

---

[1] Based on a forty-hour work week times forty-eight effective work weeks minus vacation and holidays over forty years.

headed by following your North Star is important. However, what's more important is whether you are the one steering the ship. Are you headed in that direction because you made the decision for yourself? Or are you following your parents' decision? Or are you being guided by your culture or social perspectives? I encourage you to be honest with yourself when you answer these questions. If you realize you didn't make the decision yourself, then it's time you realize…

You have options

The degree you chose provides you with options. As a computer science student, I thought there were only two job options: developer or network administrator. I never really considered the variety of other jobs that my degree allowed me to do. I thought my choice was basically made, so I focused on my studies. I did not get involved in many school clubs or volunteer much. My only saving grace was being part of a co-op program, which was instrumental in gaining experience. SIWIKE would have been to explore the options that were out there and to examine what would have been suitable for me.

As an example, if you take a degree in accounting, you may limit your potential career path to the most obvious: working for one of the Big Four accounting firms. But there are many other applications of accounting knowledge — audit, tax, actuarial work, bookkeeping, forensics, and advisory roles. (And so on.) You'll find that each degree has many nuances. And arts and humanities degrees like psychology and sociology have an even broader application — graduates fit well into many jobs and roles.

Another consideration is what industry to work in. You could be an accountant at one of the Big Four or an accountant at a hospital. So even if you decide to be an accountant, you should realize that the choice has many options that could be refined.

Experience your options; refine your choices

If you take the time to refine your career options, how do you know what's a good choice? If a good choice is measured by how good you are at it, how much you can get paid for it, and how much you like it, then that's what you should be experimenting with during your time at post-secondary school.

Let's start by looking at how good you are at it. That's measured by your grade point average (GPA), right? Well GPA might be an indicator, but it does not necessarily align with the real world. I know many people who were at the top of their class but did not end up as successful as other lower-scoring classmates that had other, more diverse skills. That's where things like internships, co-op terms, and other work-integrated learning (WIL) experiences come into play. You will need to gain experience in your craft and demonstrate that you can not only do the work, but you can excel at it.

Work experience can be challenging to get in today's competitive market. Starting with volunteer work is a great way to put your skills into practice and get precious experience. I know that volunteering to help campus recruiting efforts added a lot of value to my career, as doing the work for free allowed me to gain experience that I would not have been paid to gain elsewhere.

Does that sound like a lot of work? Perhaps. But by doing so, you can explore your options. If working part-time to pay for school limits your options, you might have to be creative and make the most out of the options you do have.

I thought that I had already made my choice for my future job/career and couldn't choose anything different. Out of the two roles I saw myself in, coder and network administrator, I got a role as a network administrator for my first two co-op terms. I really wanted a coder role for my second one. I ended up being disappointed, instead getting a position as an associate technical consultant. Which, in hindsight, was probably the best thing that could have happened to me. I was forced to explore out of sheer luck.

SIWIKE means being more proactive about the options and choices your degree affords. For a bit of inspiration, look at the alumni of your school and program to see what they are doing. Use alumni resources or social media networks. Look at last year's graduates and compare them to those that graduated a few years, half a decade ago or more. Which ones are doing things that are enticing and appealing to you? They were in your shoes a few years ago, so their current path is likely within your realm of possibility. You can expand outside alumni to others from other schools who graduated from similar programs. Explore. And don't worry so much about finding the perfect role as you should realize that...

Your choice is not permanent

My dad worked at IBM for over thirty years. He received long-service awards for various milestones. That type of singly focused dedication does not seem to be as common any more. Even with just twelve years of experience at Deloitte, I was considered "old" in the group I worked with. One thing that I did end up doing well was growing and adapting my skills and experiences.

After realizing that I wasn't fond of coding, I decided to seek out opportunities that would give me different experiences. I took the experience and skills I gained in one place and looked to build on them while steering myself in another direction.

Now that doesn't mean you must do the same. It just means that you need to understand that you have a choice. With the pace of change today, it might not be a choice and may become a necessity in order to stay relevant.

TRY THIS: Explore your choices

As you're taking your courses, take some time to reflect on what parts of the work you are finding enjoyable and what you are good at. See if you can explore those skills through paid experience (co-op placements, internships, or whatever you have available to you). If you can't get paid for the work, volunteer. And if all else fails, then see if you can start a side project to test out those skills and gain experience in the real world. Reflect on the experiences you are getting and refine your choices.

Use some of your NN-time to reflect weekly, or daily if you can. And some of your NN-time to explore these choices and add to your personal investment time as well!

Up next...

Use your priority time to explore what is out there. Go beyond the classroom to explore. Paid work experience is the best representation of what the working world will be like after graduation. Volunteer work is the next best thing. Side projects can be beneficial as well.

Now that you're making the time to explore and refine your choices, don't forget about why you're in school in the first place...

Career success starts with school success

I wasn't a very good student — at least, not in my first year. In high school, I had taken many of the courses that would be used for university marks in my second-last year, and my last year of high school was elective heavy, which made for a lighter workload. And after the marks were in, my motivation dwindled and I developed a bit of a slacker attitude—"slacktitude" according to the urban dictionary. I carried this attitude into university. Some of those habits still sit with me. SIWIKE means building good habits for future success.

Keep in mind that marks aren't necessarily a predictor of work success. But a lot can be said about treating school as a testing ground for future success. When I provide feedback on people's resumes, I often recommend focusing on activities rather than achievements. (Activities are what you did: took a course, finished an assignment. Achievements are how well you did: the grade you got in that course and on that assignment.) In reality, the difference between activities and achievements starts with an exercise in understanding expectations. Then meeting or exceeding those expectations—adapting to new circumstances, assessing competing priorities, calculating needs versus wants, finding or creating motivation. These are all the skills that will be important to have when working in an actual job.

It's also important to note that writing your resume should start now, even if you're graduating years from now. Why? Let's imagine you are now a few weeks from graduation and are getting ready to enter the real world. You figure, now is the time to sit down to write your resume. You write down your name and contact information, then your school, program, and GPA. Then what? It's hard to write more on your resume when you don't have experiences to put down. The days when a degree meant a job on graduation are long gone. This means that school success is not just about what happens during class or your marks. It also includes having experiences that set you up for success and allow you to gain subsequent experiences (e.g., in future jobs).

One of the most important SIWIKE I found in school is what Dr. Carol Dweck calls a "growth mindset." When I started school, I had the opposite, what's called a "fixed mindset." A fixed mindset is when you believe that what you can change is limited: You were born with a certain IQ and therefore can only be so smart. You were born with a certain level of artistic talent, so you can only draw so well. When I was growing up, what didn't help me was that I thought I was smart. I was labelled gifted because I did well on a few tests. Which is not bad on its own, but unfortunately, I let it get to my head. I developed poor studying habits (i.e, the habit of not studying). After all, everyone said I was smart, so why did I need to study? Oh, how naïve I was as I didn't realize smart is a relative term. I was *supposed* to be smart but when the world progresses and you don't, the world catches up. I was also getting further and further behind because I wasn't willing to put in the work to stay smart.

Luckily, I stumbled into a "growth mindset," which presumes that you can improve (see the Self-Awareness section of this book in Chapter 2 to read how the stumble happened). By gaining more knowledge and applying that knowledge to develop new skills you can increase your IQ. By learning techniques and practising, you can become a better artist. And studying is how people become smarter, not just by sitting there pretending they know everything. ("I know" was one of my favourite phrases as a kid.)

Why is doing well in post-secondary studies so important? For one, employers need a way of comparing those candidates that are coming straight out of post-secondary school. As a benchmark, they don't have much else to go on other than your grades. The standard is set based on the volume of applications received. Out of hundreds of applications they only have the time to interview let's say five people per role. And if you're not above that cut-off threshold, unlucky number six ... then sorry. If you just can't seem to achieve that GPA, it's not the end of the world. You could alternatively become a *practitioner* of your craft to validate whether you can actually do the work but you're just not good at taking tests. See the Network & Build Meaningful Connections section of this book (Chapter 10) to walk through finding that alternate route.

Still don't feel doing well in school is important? Another way I think of school is that it is years of deliberate practice for people who don't know what they want to do with their lives and haven't yet been inspired.

Deliberate practice is what's left out of Malcolm Gladwell's 10,000-hour rule, popularized in his book *Outliers*. To paraphrase, the 10,000-hour rule says that you can be exceptional—world-class—at something, pretty much anything, with 10,000 hours of practice. That translates to roughly ten years of almost full-time practice. The amendment I want to add to that statement is that the majority, if not all, of that practice should be *deliberate* practice. Deliberate practice comes from the original research of Malcom Gladwell's rule, which was done by Anders Ericsson. Simply put, deliberate practice is practice with the purpose of learning and improving. As an example, with the 10,000-hour rule, if you play tennis for ten years, then you'd get close to world-class performance. Most tennis amateurs know that's not true. But taking that practice with the intent of improving your forehand one day, your backhand the next, your serve the following, then footwork, then all the other skills needed to make a great tennis player, the deliberate practice will achieve world-class results. Keep in mind applying deliberate practice does not necessarily mean you will become number one in the world, as there are some deliberate practice and improvement techniques that are better than others, plus biology plays a factor. But it does mean you could get into the top percentile of tennis players. In addition, often people aren't self-aware enough to know what changes to make, and a coach can be vital to help them see what they're doing with an external eye.

So how does school become deliberate practice? Let's face it, going to class and doing tests and assignments are not most people's idea of fun. You could be out having fun rather than going to class, doing homework, or studying for exams. But, if you change your perspective to view the effort as "deliberate practice" for your future career, you might find yourself more motivated. Think about it. If you can apply some discipline to do well in something you only like, imagine how far you could go in pursuit of something you love? Imagine you go to class and pay attention. When completing your homework, work at understanding how it could be applied to your future job. And study for exams to get a sense of how well you might have learned. Perhaps in doing these things you should also be navigating yourself, and be attempting to find the things that you are more interested in, more passionate about. Once you've applied deliberate practice to studies you are less than passionate about, imagine applying that same mindset and effort to something that you are truly interested in doing. So, until you find your drive and passion, at the very least, get through school. Explore through school. Better still, do well in school, and you'll be sure to set yourself up for success in the future.

TRY THIS: Reflect on your past accomplishments

Life is supposed to be a marathon, and school seemed to me to be a series of sprints: go to class, cram, get tested, take a holiday break, repeat. Do you find that there is barely enough time to catch your breath before the next term starts? SIWIKE that I encourage is to take time to reflect for the purposes of learning and for documenting. Reflect to learn what went well and how you can do more, as well as what didn't go so well and how you could avoid that. It will not be possible to avoid everything, but it's worth a try to avoid some of it. The documenting part is writing down what you did; you've probably done this more than you think. When you're just about to graduate and need to write down all your activities and accomplishments, your memory might fail you. Taking the time, even as little as fifteen minutes every term, to document what you've done will make the process easier. Use your NN-time or schedule separate time to do so. A simple hack is to create a calendar appointment that recurs every four months (at the end of each term) without a stop date. When the reminder pops up, don't negotiate with yourself. Take the next opportunity to reflect, learn, and document all that you've accomplished during your school years. You'll thank yourself for it later. Perhaps when you sit down to finally write that resume.

Up next...

You're amazing! And if you don't feel amazing yet, make a mental note that you are becoming amazing. You've prioritized yourself, started making your own choices and you're becoming successful at school. Reflect to learn and document. An occasional point of reflection might be to confirm whether post-secondary education is right for you.

Post-secondary education isn't for everyone — and that's okay

Learning is important. Getting an education is important. However, school is not necessarily the path that will help you get that learning and education. Many people can learn faster and better outside of a school environment, while some people need the structure and the constant oversight that a school environment provides.

Your parents may hate me for writing this section, but you may need to seriously assess if school is right for you. School is often for prestige, sometimes not even your own prestige. Occasionally, it's so that parents can say that they provided well for their son or daughter by putting them through top schools. School can be great. And for most people, it's probably the best place to start. For others, there are other ways to learn.

To be successful, you might not need that formal school education. Many people learn from the school of hard knocks, and just figure out what they need to. You might be in the minority where your hustle and street smarts, instead of classrooms and textbooks, may be the key to your success. Although I've observed that minority growing with all the resources for learning available through the internet and elsewhere. If you are fuelled by passion to do other things *and* you're okay with not honouring your parents' wishes for you to attend school, then you might consider an alternative education. Otherwise, you should probably make the most out of your school experience and use it as an opportunity to find that passion, and then do whatever you want! And my hopes are that the school system eventually changes to support more of this type of learning.

If you are thinking that school is not right for you, then it's important to be honest with yourself. Bill Gates and Mark Zuckerberg are some famous "drop outs," which is a misunderstood fact. They did not drop out of school; they took a leave from studying to pursue something they loved and could have returned if that opportunity did not work out. Luckily for them, their Microsoft and Facebook decisions worked out. They moved towards something they loved, versus away from something they didn't.

Perhaps a question will help: If you weren't in school, what would you be doing that you would love, that provides value to the world, that you're good at, and that you could get paid for? If you can't answer that question, then school is probably the right place for you. If you can answer the question, then taste it first. See if it's really for you. And if you find that it is, what are you waiting for? Go do it!

TRY THIS: Explore something on the side

For those of you who are born entrepreneurs, you won't be very successful or happy in the traditional school environment. You're probably already doing something on the side. Don't confuse not being successful or happy at school with being a born entrepreneur. What you may want to do is taste entrepreneurship and get some experience in the work by starting something while you're still in school — selling stuff online, mowing lawns around the neighbourhood, tutoring, or whatever else you can think of. Try it and learn the entrepreneurial skills. If you have access to entrepreneurial programs like a start-up incubator, then see if you can join one and get some help. Measure your success at entrepreneurship and at school. Challenge yourself to do well in school while being successful with your start-up. If your start-up is successful, then you have the choice to focus more time on it to make it even more successful. If it isn't successful, then entrepreneurship might not have been the right thing for you anyways, and you have school to fall back on. But you'll probably have had a bunch of experiences that will give you a good sense of what you want to do in the future. Or at least what you don't want to do.

Up next...

You've started building a foundation for future career success by prioritizing yourself, knowing your options, making choices and taking time to explore. Next, it's time to think about what success even means. Defining success is an important part of achieving it.

Evaluate what success means to you

In university, I never really thought about what success meant. I thought it meant finishing university, getting a job, and eventually settling down and getting married. All of that American-dream, white-picket-fence stuff.

When I got a job, success to me was associated with salary. The more I made, the more successful I was. This mindset started getting annoying as I progressed in my career. I was in one of those jobs where I was paid in the potential for making the big bucks later. There I was, working sometimes twice as much as my friends *AND* making less. I was learning more, sure, having broader and sometimes deeper experiences, and potentially making more meaningful and useful connections than many of my peers, but those weren't part of my measures of success. It was only on my journey to start my own business and found FOCUS Inspired® where I truly understood that success wasn't just measured by dollars in a bank account. That change in perspective was profound.

You have likely seen and heard stories of so-called successful people who seem to have more money than they know what to do with, but who end up in a tragedy, some to the point of taking their own lives because they aren't fulfilled. You may have also heard stories of people who don't have many material possessions but are insanely happy and are inspired to live each day to the fullest. An interesting thought experiment is: which would you rather be?

The hopeful answer is: Why choose? Why not aim to be successful and fulfilled? One approach is to find what fulfills you and turn it into something that is valuable to others. When you provide value to others the money will follow. This approach might be different from the typical path of earning enough money so that eventually you can do what fulfills you. Starting with fulfillment is harder than it looks and often begins with being content with what you have.

Although it is important to be content with what you have, you should always want more. This might seem to be a bit of a contradiction, but in this case "more" isn't in material possessions. You should at least want more of yourself — to constantly seek to improve, to constantly add value to the lives of others, to grow your "fulfillment bank account."

With those thoughts in mind, take a moment to think about what success is for you. Is graduation important to you? Or is it more for your parents? How about getting a job in a certain field? Making a certain amount of money? Having a certain title? Or making an impact? Or is your success dependent on your parents' happiness even if that comes at the expense of your own?

What if you are only pursuing your current schooling to appease someone else but really want to be doing something else? Does that mean you're stuck? Each household has different circumstances, but I hope that most of your parents just want you to be able to take care of yourself. They likely have a vision that the current degree will lead to being able to provide for yourself and your future family (usually consisting of their future grandkids) and ultimately lead to your own happiness. They may not understand the entrepreneurial path, or that being a creative, or whatever it is that you're called to pursue, can be a career option. One approach could be to show them that you can be successful. Spend 9 a.m. to 5 p.m. (or whatever equivalent school hours you have) appeasing them by attending and doing well at school, then 5 p.m. to 12 a.m. showing them that you can be happy and successful following another path. (And yes, you can sleep from 12 a.m. to 9 a.m). Might that come at the expense of time with friends, Netflix, and video games? Perhaps, and what are the alternatives? Living a life for the happiness of your parents and not for yourself? Or being selfish and thinking of just yourself? The main point is that you have a choice. Seek professional guidance on what the right course of action might be for your situation, and do realize there are options.

Who is more successful: someone who works themselves to the bone for a $200,000 salary and complains from Monday to Friday? Or someone who makes a $40,000 salary that allows them to be happy and fulfilled at work and provide for their family while leaving enough to take a nice vacation every few years?

At the end of the day, you want to be the one setting your own vision of success. You make the choice. This means you should take the time during university to validate your North Star and chart your course for career success. And perhaps you could be happy and fulfilled at work while eventually turning that into a $200,000 salary.

TRY THIS: Validate your North Star

In choosing your degree, you made a decision that will stick with you for years, perhaps decades. Given that extended time frame, don't you think validating the decision would be worthwhile? If you do, how might you do that? One way would be to research the paths of five people who are where you want to be. (More if you want to be more thorough in your research.) Meet with them to learn what excites them about their work and see if that resonates with you. Find stepping stones in their journey to see whether you have them in your plan. Look for ways you can gain similar experiences sooner rather than later. Validate that those experiences are aligned with your current North Star. If not, adjust your North Star appropriately. That adjustment might not be easy, but it might be necessary if you really want to reach your potential. You owe it to yourself to unlock all the greatness inside of you.

As a note, there will be a lot of connecting with people in the *TRY THIS* sections throughout the book. If you don't think you're good at networking and building connections, I'll give you some useful insights that helped me in a later section and you can come back to this challenge armed with new tools. But make sure you do come back and practise making connections as you'll probably find, just as I did, that who you know is often more important than what you know.

Up next...

You've spent a bit of time reflecting on your definition of success, and started incorporating a few tools to get out there. Now you get into finding out more about yourself!

Chapter 2: Who Are You and What Do You Want?

I was a computer scientist in training. Then I was a technologist. Then a management consultant in sourcing and procurement. At the same time, I was a campus recruiter. I thought I knew who I was and what I wanted. While I was immersed in self-reflection, I realized that the things I was paid to do weren't me. And worse still, I didn't really know what I wanted. What I wanted at the time was influenced by the people and the environment around me, which would have been fine if they all aligned, but I realized I had to be honest with myself if I wanted to shine.

Are you a chef or cook?[2]

I grew up in an environment where school was a given. Graduating high school was a requirement. Graduating university was expected. Getting a job after work was a necessity. It seemed like a standard recipe and a universal norm. Does that sound familiar for you? Many people I've spoken to have a similar recipe for themselves. But did that recipe come from themselves or was it handed to them? Was it from parents or peers? Somewhere else? The recipe calls for a kilo of good grades with a side of hard work, and out comes a tasty career dish. Just follow the recipe and you'll be fine. A cook does that. However, you have the option of living as a chef. A chef creates. There is no recipe. A chef looks at the ingredients available and tests what might pair well together, what might enhance or overpower another flavour. A chef takes what is given to them and makes it into something unique and magical. And everyone has the opportunity to be a chef, to take their career and their lives and make it truly, uniquely them.

Being a chef is not mutually exclusive with being a cook. You could be part chef and part cook. Be more chef by experimenting with different ways of learning or gaining experience, or be more cook by following what school or other traditional ways have provided. It's up

---

[2] Inspiration came from Tim Urban's blog *Wait But Why*. https://waitbutwhy.com/2015/11/the-cook-and-the-chef-musks-secret-sauce.html

to you. There may be circumstances in your career that compel you to be more like a cook. That's fine as long as it works for you. Complete your degree while doing what you love on the side. Cook by day, chef by night. Finish your degree and get a good job, and after you've stabilized, take an opportunity to explore your passion. You might cook to learn the business then venture out on your own as a chef. It's up to you. And I hope that you understand being a cook or chef is an analogy to how much you follow pre-set notions on career progress, and that I'm not literally telling you to be a cook or a chef. Though you could if you want; I just wanted to set the record straight. Cool? Alright.

Another useful analogy is comparing a bus driver and a taxi driver. Both help you get to your destination. The bus starts at the station. Goes to the first stop (school), the next stop (job), the next stop (promotion), and so on, until you eventually get to your destination. The taxi may take a back alley (an unconventional education), a shortcut through a sketchy neighbourhood (a less-than-glamorous job or a fulfilling volunteer opportunity for the less fortunate or a boss that might be pushing the boundaries of what's ethical), then through the side streets of a posh neighbourhood (a cushy job with smart people) to get you to your destination. Again, you have a choice to take the set, prescribed route, or find a different way to your career destinations.

Most people mistakenly assume that I use the analogy of the cook / chef and bus driver / taxi driver to mean that they *must* become metaphorical chefs and taxi drivers. I only use this analogy to help people understand that those options are out there. Many people assume that there is only one path and that they must follow that path to achieve their goals. For those who have not yet found their purpose, following what society deems as the recipe for success is a good option. *But* you have the option to go off-recipe or off-route when you have a purpose that aligns with that direction. It's your choice. Each choice has consequences, sometimes good, sometimes bad. Sometimes the consequence seems good at first then ends up being bad. And sometimes the consequence seems bad at first and ends up being great. Once more for good measure: it's your choice.

Going off and doing something that isn't traditional doesn't mean you should do so foolishly. Many successful people have backup plans when they go off-recipe because they understand that the path in front of them won't necessarily be easy or convenient. Bill Gates is reported to have dropped out of school, but what is less-known is that he did so on a leave of absence so that he could return to school if things didn't work out, and he had family that he could fall back on as well. Richard Branson started Virgin Airlines with a contract from the airplane manufacturer that stated he could return the airplanes if it didn't work out.

I encourage you to move one notch or two towards the chef / taxi driver side of the spectrum to try to challenge yourself to chart a course where you can reach your career potential. Try something new. Get out of your comfort zone. Sit in the front row. You never know what great experiences you might be missing.

TRY THIS: Find what dish you want to create

Whether you want to be a chef or a cook, it's useful to equip yourself with common skills. Find someone who has successfully created the dish you like. Their online profiles will often have a high-level outline of the recipe they used to get them to where they are. Connect with them and see if they are willing to share their secret spice blend. Some chefs will be willing to share, others may not. Those profiles will be the recipe to get to where they got to. You may want to replicate the same recipe or incorporate flavours from someone else's journey.

After connecting, reflect on how to do a better job connecting, and plan which improvements you will actually implement in future interactions.

Up next...

Understanding that you don't have to follow a set recipe or a prescribed bus route was freeing for me. Getting to really know yourself and becoming self-aware even more so. So, let's get on with it!

Self-awareness is everything

Up until now, we've set aside NN-time for you to invest in yourself, made you aware of the choice you have, and encouraged you to try other things. However, if I had to pick one strategy to help ensure success on your career journey, it would be to develop self-awareness. Most people are aware of their surroundings and the external world they interact with. Their senses help them react appropriately to them.

However, most are not actually aware of what is going on inside themselves that causes these reactions. Awareness of your choices, your strengths and weaknesses, and the reasons for your reactions is important to boost self-awareness. The rest of this section is designed to help you get to know yourself.

When I was in university, I think I was too smart for my own good. My own arrogance made it difficult to be self-aware. I recall a breakthrough in my third year. Up until then, I was quite introverted, mostly keeping to myself. There were study-cubes at school (desks with boards on three sides to give you privacy for studying — apparently, they are called carrels). This was my routine: I would go to class, find a carrel, go to class, find another carrel, then class, then carrel. Maybe some lunch. Class, carrel, class again. Then I made my way home. I did that pretty much every day from my first year to my third year. Sometime in third year, I had what I call my WTF moment, where I said to myself, "What the f*@#? Is this what my life has amounted to?" I decided to make something more out of my life. I decided to have a conversation with the person in the next study carrel. And that conversation ... totally sucked! It was super awkward! I remember a quote that I wanted to live by: "I never lose. I either win or I learn." The awkward conversation might have been a loss, but I don't lose. It definitely wasn't a win (it was super awkward). So, what did I learn? Well, first, you can't just jump into a conversation midstride; you want to break the ice first. The next conversation was better. And the one after was better still. And so on.

That might not have been the first time I had a flash of self-awareness, but it was the first time that I was self-aware enough to realize that it was okay that I wasn't good at something (in this case networking and more fundamentally having a conversation), and then do something about it. It was the first time I was aware of being in a growth mindset. Self-awareness isn't a switch that turns on or off. It's much more like a muscle that you need to exercise. First, I had to reflect back on times when I should have been more self-aware. Then occasionally, I was able to catch myself in a similar moment and adjust my behaviour. Even now, I don't catch myself all the time, but it's more frequent than before. Practice makes permanent.

An important part of self-awareness is understanding the identity you give yourself. In that identity, the perspective you take has a profound impact on your future success. Self-awareness asks you to understand your thoughts and realize that you can shape them to better serve you. A positive outlook on life can be hard to maintain, but those who can maintain one are more successful.

I heard a folk tale about twin girls that had an alcoholic father. They were studied over the course of their lives to research differences in their behaviours. The first girl was a poor student, very rebellious, got into a lot of fights, into drugs, and ended up homeless on the streets. When asked why she ended up where she did, she said, "Because my father was an alcoholic." The second twin was an exceptional student, followed her passion, achieved a lot in her community, and found a very successful career, amassing a lot of wealth in the process. When asked why she ended up where she did, she said, "Because my father was an alcoholic." So, are you telling yourself you are a victim of your circumstances or are you an architect of your future? Being aware of your negative thoughts, and reducing them by replacing them with positive thoughts will be important in future success.

TRY THIS: Set aside time to build self-awareness

Spending some of your NN-time on self-reflection can do wonders for your self-awareness. Looking for patterns and their causes can help you understand yourself better.

We are often unaware of our strengths and faults, so asking trusted friends and family can also help increase your self-awareness. Getting honest feedback from others can be tough since friends might worry about hurting your feelings or damaging your relationship. That means you might need to spend time making sure you will be open to accepting their feedback. It may hurt, but it's better to hurt a little now, then to have the hurt compounded as time passes.

Up next...

The journey to self-awareness starts with the first step and continues one step at a time. Learning foundational elements about yourself like your tendency to meet expectations will help you make progress in getting to know yourself.

Know your own tendencies

Throughout school I procrastinated by playing video games, watching TV — all sorts of distractions would occupy my time. I'm glad YouTube and Facebook weren't as pervasive back then or I probably would have been much worse off. Sometimes I could motivate myself to get stuff done, but unfortunately, much of the time these distractions got the better of me. Still, I usually managed to get through things, and I knew that this was important. I didn't really make a focused effort to understand how I could be most effective at completing essential tasks until after I started working. As a management consultant, I had a lot of work to do. I realized that when I told people what I was doing and when it would be done, I was far more likely to do it than if I kept it to myself.

Only this year (2017) did I find Gretchen Rubin's book *Better Than Before*. The book outlines four tendencies that describe how different people meet expectations. Whether you are more motivated by inner or outer expectations informs which of the four tendency categories you fall into. I found I was an Obliger, which means that if I set expectations for myself, I was less likely to hit them versus if others had expectations of me. On the opposite side are Questioners, who need inner justification for the importance of a task, and without it, even other people's expectations aren't enough to motivate them. Most people are one of these two tendencies. There is a small minority who are Upholders, those who meet expectations whether they set it or other people set it. And a smaller percent of the population are Rebels, those who do things on their own time. For Rebels, there is sometimes no rational way they can convince themselves they need to do something; stuff only gets done when they feel like it.

Rubin's book was published in 2015, so it couldn't have been SIWIKE for me when I was in school. Yet I encourage you to read this book and explore your tendencies, as it could be SIWIKE for you. Even now, the concepts have helped me motivate myself more readily. I have consumed much information on habits, but of everything I've read, *Better Than Before* seems to have the most practical guidance, strategies, tactics, and hacks to get you to be better than before.

SIWIKE I took away from much of the habit research is that everyone is different, and their tendencies are different in different contexts. What I have found for myself is that I am one tendency in a work context, another in a personal context while relating to others, and yet another in a personal context related to my own expectations. One of the things I've learned is to not beat myself up when I don't meet expectations. Instead, I take the time to learn what I can do the next time around to make myself more effective.

TRY THIS: Know your tendencies

Take some time to reflect on times when you met expectations and got stuff done versus those times when you missed expectations and didn't get something done. See if you can identify if you had inner expectations (it was important to you so you got it done) or outer expectations (you knew it was important to someone else so you got it done), a combination of both, or if stuff only got done when you felt like it. You will see patterns emerge in different contexts, be it at work, in your personal life, with a certain group of people, or in certain situations. Use those patterns to make yourself better for future situations.

Pick up a copy of *Better Than Before* for more detailed tips and tricks. To learn what your tendency is, complete the Tendencies quiz here: https://gretchenrubin.com/books/the-four-tendencies/take-the-quiz. If the link changes, you'll likely find the quiz link with a quick Google search.

Up next...

The next step to knowing yourself is finding what your superpower is. And yes, you do have a superpower — something you do better than others around you, perhaps even better than most of the world. Keep in mind that it might not be one thing; it could be the intersection of a few strengths that together act as your superpower.

Focus on your strengths; make your weaknesses irrelevant

In school, I wanted to be the best at everything. I did well academically. In elementary school I thought I was a natural. It was easier to be good among a small group. In high school, it was harder to be good as there were just more people. I was quite creative and good at teaching others and I was decent at math and science. I wasn't great at music. I still wanted to be the best at everything, so I tried to improve the things I wasn't great at to make up for my shortcomings. Turns out those things were shortcomings for a reason. I wasn't good at them and I didn't really like them.

Take music. I was strongly encouraged to pick up an instrument (particularly strong Asian parent encouragement). I picked up guitar because it seemed cool. I started playing and instantly I knew that I sucked and didn't really like it. I didn't have the motivation to learn, and I wasted a bunch of time going through the motions and not getting much better. Learning music was a definite weakness. Contrast that with my current thirst for learning. If I haven't consumed some new content over the course of the day, I don't feel as if it was a good day. On good days, I have learned something new that I might apply to improve myself or someone else in the future. On great days, I've shared that knowledge to improve the quality of someone else's life.

With my experience with music and with helping others, I've realized that talent is a thing. People are naturally inclined to certain things. Look at the various twin studies out there and you can see that people are genetically predisposed to a variety of things from physical abilities to tendencies for addiction. Then there are environmental factors: where and how you grew up. And there are experiential factors: what you put into practice and habituate. There are various concepts that align with these strategies, and I like to refer to the book *Now, Discover Your Strengths* by Marcus Buckingham and Donald O. Clifton who explain that your strengths are made up of your talent, your knowledge, and your skills. They have a list of thirty-four talent themes. The number is less important than understanding that you have more than one talent. The more interesting concept is — instead of looking to fix your weaknesses — to become a well-rounded person, double down on your strengths and make your weaknesses irrelevant. Let's break it down.

Talent is your innate ability, what you were prewired to do well. The higher your talent it is, the closer you are to being "world-class." That wiring can be rerouted through knowledge, which is the education that you gain (i.e., reading the books to understand the theory — as in reading a book about how to play better golf), and through skill, the training and execution you put in (e.g., putting the theory to real-life practice — as in going to the driving range and practising on an actual golf course). According to the book, all of these things contribute to your strengths.

So, as you assess your strengths, understand that some may be hidden or underrepresented. Putting more effort and focus on developing your knowledge and skill of the talent might uncover something surprising.

Consider someone evaluating the development of three strengths. We start with talent. There are assessment tools that help you break down talents into various categories —"Strengths Finder" is one of the broadest. It was created through the Gallup company (they are known for doing surveys using The Gallup Poll), and it breaks down talents into thirty-four different variations. We'll just use three for illustration. In this case, a score of 10 is world-class and a score of 1 is not talented at all.

Strength	Talent Level
A	5
B	10
C	3

Figure 1: Strength example — sample talent levels

Let's spend some time on each strength. Again, for illustration purposes, we'll consider the multiplier for knowledge as the number of years learning or studying and skill as the number of years training or executing. Let's put it in a scenario:

Strength	Talent Level	Knowledge Level	Skill Level	Strength Value
A	5	8	5	**200**
B	10	1	1	10
C	3	4	5	60

Figure 2: Strength scenario 1

This person spent a long time learning and practising strength A, one which was a mediocre talent, and eventually developed that strength to a hypothetical strength value of 200.

Based on the amount of talent this person had in strength B, they could have developed it into a world-class strength, but for whatever reason they didn't spend much time on it — perhaps they only found out about it recently — and they only achieved a strength value of 10.

They spent some time developing strength C, in which they might have been the worst — probably to try to be well-rounded — and they achieved some level of competency, with a strength value of 60.

Let's look at another scenario, which has the same talents, but we will swap out the time spent gaining the knowledge and practising the skill.

Strength	Talent Level	Knowledge Level	Skill Level	Strength Value
A	5	4	5	100
B	10	8	5	400
C	3	1	1	3

Figure 3: Strength scenario 2

Here, the time spent on acquiring knowledge and skills correlates better with the person's natural talent level, and without expending any extra time we've doubled the strength value.

Now let's characterize these talents as A: related to business / accounting, B: related to creativity / design, and C: related to science / engineering.

- In scenario 1 with strength A having the highest investment in knowledge / skill, the person might have been directed to take their schooling in business / accounting (strength A). They studied and practised in their field. They didn't do much in creativity / design (strength B) because their parents didn't think it was a stable career. They did some science / engineering (strength C) and they got through high school but did not pursue it further.

- In scenario 2, with strength B having the highest investment in knowledge / skill, the same person might have had parents that allowed them to follow their talent. They found that they were natural at creativity / design (strength B) and focused their attention there rather than investing time in business (strength A) like their alternate reality self. And they put little attention into their science / engineering (strength C), where they had very little talent.

Now we could have easily swapped A, B, and C around and said that someone forced into creative work should have been in business, or any other combination, but I assume you see the point.

These scenarios are an oversimplification. They are based on anecdotes and my experience with my clients and are used as an illustrative example. The notions about talent came from discussions I've heard about inconsistencies in the so-called 10,000-hour rule, which can exist often if a person didn't get the proper knowledge or training for their particular set of talents and missed out on capitalizing on their full potential. And to put it all in a numeric formula oversimplifies all of the possible variables for effects of nature and nurture experienced by someone. But hopefully the concept comes across.

The main point is that you often need to explore to see if something is really a talent and to see if it could be developed into a strength. To reach your career potential, you need to first try, then develop and see where that takes you.

All-time great college basketball coach John Wooden once said, "Success is peace of mind, which is a direct result of self-satisfaction in knowing you made the effort to do your best to become the best that you are capable of becoming." Imagine a scenario in which you're drifting through life. Your studies aren't engaging, and you do the bare minimum to get by. You get okay grades, but you know that you could have achieved more if you put in the effort. Now imagine a scenario where you decide not to drift. You give it your all to engage in your studies. You put in the effort to do the best you can. Now replace "studies" with anything else — volunteer work, extracurricular activities, relationships with friends. Why wouldn't you make the best out of each opportunity provided to you and become the best you are capable of becoming?

Now, if we must, let's move on to weaknesses. Weaknesses are those areas in which you don't excel — those things that often make you self-conscious, perhaps even hold you back. I like to say that a weakness is something that makes you feel weaker, that drains you of your energy, and perhaps even of your happiness. If we use this definition, then you do want to work on your weaknesses, but not necessarily until they become strengths. You want to work on them to the point where they are basically neutral and effectively irrelevant. If a weakness is not draining your energy, nor contributing positively to it, it just is. Take communication, for example. As humans are naturally social beings, communication is important. And it is important at different levels to different people based on their circumstances. If you are a stereotypical introvert, that doesn't mean you are incapable of communicating. It just means that some forms of communication, such as randomly initiating conversations or engaging in small talk, do not come naturally to you, and will therefore be harder for you to do. And when you must communicate in that way, you feel more drained. If you get a job in customer service, then you will need to train yourself to the point where the energy drain you experience is nonexistent or at least as minimal as possible. Or consider finding roles where you are using forms of communication that are comfortable to you, and you can spend more time focusing on your strengths.

Using a similar definition, a strength is something that makes you feel stronger, something that gives you energy and possibly happiness. So, if you focus more on your strengths and make your weaknesses irrelevant you will be spending your time on things that give you energy and happiness. You will see how much your life could improve.

You know when you've hit on a potential strength when you reach a state of flow. Flow states are when you feel in the zone. You lose track of time and have a sense of internal reward during or after the experience. Take time to reflect on when you reach these flow states and see if you can find patterns. Where a flow state happens, a strength is often close by.

TRY THIS: Learn new skills and improve old ones

Take the time to assess your strengths. Reflect on those times when you felt strong. How can you get more out of those times? How can you invest time to further improve? How can you apply your strengths to different contexts and situations? Reflect on times when you felt weak. How can you reduce the time you spend doing things that make you feel weak?

Also, take the time to explore skills you've never acquired before. At any stage of life, there are always experiences you haven't yet had and things you can do that you haven't yet done that could help you find potential strengths.

Up next...

It's okay if you have no idea what your strengths are or what your superpower is. Making a conscious decision to improve through cultivating your interests and passions will eventually help you discover what they are. Or at least you'll have fun trying to figure it out!

Your value lies in your passions

I did a degree in computer science and was good at it. I applied my understanding of technology to business to become a management consultant and was good at it. I had those strengths. However, there was a problem: I didn't love it. I wasn't passionate about it. I've had many conversations about finding or following your passion. How does someone do that? The simplest way is to start with an interest. The interest itch is scratched. That itch compels you to build on your interest more and more until one day, it ignites into a passion. You may be encouraged to do what you love. Steve Jobs, the late founder of Apple computers, is famous for saying in one of his commencement speeches "the only way to do great work is to love what you do." He says "love what you do" not "do what you love" — a subtle yet profound difference.

The ignition time varies, and it may never happen — you may never love what you do. But as you gain experience and mastery, that interest could turn into a passion. If you shape the experience and focus on the areas you're most excited about, you're actually creating your passion rather than finding or following it.

Knowing what you're good at (your strengths) and what you love (your passions) may not be useful if it does not generate value. The intersection of all are outlined in the concept of *ikigai*. *Ikigai* is a

Japanese concept which roughly translates to "the reason you wake up in the morning." *Ikigai* is the intersection of four things:

- what you love to do
- what you're good at
- what the world needs
- what you can be paid for

Figure 4: Your purpose — Ikigai[3]

If you are just starting your career, *ikigai* should be the least of your worries, but it is a useful concept to understand. School will hopefully start you on the journey of discovering what you're good at. Then along the way if you explore your interests, what you like to do might turn

---

[3] The diagram was adapted from various images and representations of *ikigai* found on the web.

into what you love to do. And if during the process you find out that it's what the world needs and that you can be paid for it, then why not go for it? Another approach is to hit one of the intersections in the graph where you might be paid for what you're good at or what the word needs, for example. And with all of this, sometimes it's useful to understand your why, your purpose, to help you with your motivation.

TRY THIS: Monetize your hobbies

Hobbies are a good indicator of what you love. After all, you do them without getting paid. Could you be good at your hobby? Does the world need it and could you be paid for it? Why not find out? Finding niche communities online interested in your hobby is relatively easy. Members of these communities likely share your values. The last step is to find what they might be willing to pay for. It doesn't have to be a huge amount of money, especially if you would be doing it anyways. It might just offset your costs so you could do it more often. It might even make you a few extra dollars. Why not invest a little more time to see if you could compound the value you deliver and the dollars you earn? Then maybe you could make that hobby your job.

Up next...

Turning interests and passions into strengths and superpowers might seem elusive. If you can find a strong purpose, a strong *why*, then you can also find a way to turn those strengths into superpowers.

Find your *why* before figuring out your *how*

Your *why*, or your purpose, is at the heart of getting anything done. With a strong enough purpose, you can do anything. If I say that you must make a million dollars by the end of the year, you *might* try to make the money, but if I say if you make a million dollars by the end of the year, you will save the lives of a million babies, then you will be more motivated to do so. And if we get darker and say you must make a billion dollars or else you and your entire family will die, you will be incredibly motivated to do so. At that level, you're up 24-7 panhandling, selling off all your belongings, begging friends and family for money, and doing basically whatever it takes to make it happen. So, when you pick your goals, find a deep enough purpose and you'll achieve them.

If you want to find something you're inspired to do, it is extremely important that you find that sense of purpose. Purpose can often be derived from three areas:

- Yourself: You find purpose in doing something for yourself. You've set your own expectations and if they are met, that sense of purpose is fulfilled.

- Relationships: Your purpose rests with those around you. You are driven to do better because of the needs of family, friends, and others you are close to.

- Society: You find purpose in working for people beyond those physically close to you — to society or to the world as a whole.

None of these motivating forces are better than the others, and they are not mutually exclusive. Some people are focused on their own expectations, which is fine. Most people will feel more motivated as they move out of focusing on themselves to focusing on relationships. Then even more so if they move into a societal purpose, although that is not a requirement.

TRY THIS: Reflect on your why

Like many young professionals, I was focused on money. I did a high school co-op term where I was being paid less than university students doing the equivalent job. I got paid more money in my full-time role, but there were always people getting paid more than I was for no apparent reason. The amount I was paid was the value I delivered for the company, so having others getting paid for doing the same or sometimes even less work wasn't good for my ego. Then another realization hit: why does how much I get paid matter? Sure, it affords me the ability to buy nice things, to go to nice restaurants, and have nice experiences, but for what purpose? What impact was I having? What was I doing it for?

Here's a question: would you rather make $50,000 a year doing something you love and has a positive impact on others, or $100,000 a year doing something that is acceptable to you and doesn't really seem to make a difference? In all honesty, neither is the right answer, just as neither is the wrong answer. Let's break down the $100,000 purpose using a technique borrowed from lean manufacturing called the 5 Whys, a practice that comes from Toyota that is designed to get to the root of a problem. Instead of superficially resolving a symptom of the problem, you ask yourself a series of *why* questions with each question building from the answer to the last to try to get to the root of the issue. There are other models that go seven or ten *whys* deep, but the point is the same: to keep going until you hopefully reach the real reason.

I apply much the same principle to career development to help people discover their purpose. The idea is that the further down the *why* chain you can get, the stronger your purpose will be.

Let's go through the example with answers that came from one of my mentees:

1. Why is making a $100,000 a year salary important?

- So, that I can comfortably provide for my family.

2. Why is providing for your family important?

- What do you mean why is it important to provide for my family?!?! Because if not they'd die.

3. Well not exactly because your extended family would step in and help, or if you don't have family then you can reach out to non-profit or charitable agencies that could assist you...In any case ... Why is your family not dying important?

- So that they can carry on my legacy.

4. Why is your legacy important?

- So that I can repay the generosity of my parents and family to get to this point of my life.

At this point we got into a conversation on what legacy means to him, and we discussed concepts like making positive impact on the lives of others, being remembered at his funeral, and feeling like his life had meaning. We never got to the fourth and fifth *whys*, but the exercise helped him find a new purpose, honouring his parents and eventually becoming a role model for his children as his parents were to him. That didn't involve a $100,000 salary. It involved dedicating time to his parents and having experiences with them, helping them with causes that they are interested in and passionate about, and showing them gratitude in other ways. All this didn't end up costing him even $50,000 per year.

While writing the book, I came across other methods that go six, seven, or even more *whys* down the line, so if you're not getting the answers you're looking for, you might just be a *why* away.

Up next...

Knowing yourself and your strengths, you can start shaping your own identity. Knowing what you are known for is important to understand yourself by understanding how others perceive you.

Your purpose may be the source of your brand

Your brand in career terms is basically what you're known for, and ultimately it is how you demonstrate value. Brands such as Apple, Nike, Google, or McDonald's elicit emotions and perspectives. Those perspectives multiply the value of the brand. Many perceive those brands as having high-quality products, and their reputation makes people believe they're better than other brands that are just as good. Your personal brand might be related to your function (what you do) — "a gifted coder," "a savvy salesperson" — or to your industry (where you do it) — "a multi-faceted banking professional, "a retail guru." As you progress through your experiences, cultivating a brand can be very helpful to further yourself on that path. The brand can help provide areas of focus (i.e., you can start picking and choosing things to do based on alignment with your brand). You do have to be careful not to be totally blinded by what you may think your brand could be and lose out on opportunities, only to realize that thing you said "no" to were related to your real brand all along.

Here's a useful scenario to consider: A client at a company has a problem, and you are the first person to come to mind to solve that problem. What kind of problem is it? The type of problem the client has can indicate what your brand is.

A brand helps in the following ways:

- **Value**: People understand who you are and more importantly the help you provide. Help often comes in the form of time savings.

The knowledge and skills you have are valuable as they will save time, saving co-workers and clients from having to do whatever it is themselves. Also, keep in mind that your reputation is value based on someone's perception of you. Your tangibly delivered value might be different. And reputation is important as it is a multiplier for value.

- **Differentiation**: A brand can help set you apart from others so that someone knows to connect with you instead of someone else. Cultivating a brand is important because you want to be the first person rather than the fourth that comes to mind in a specific instance.

- **Mastery**: Knowing something inside and out shows you are a master of that domain. A brand often showcases where you have mastery or where you want to develop mastery, so you can focus your attention and efforts.

Your brand may extend outside the realm of your paid work. Volunteer activities can also express your brand. An engineer might contribute to their profession and be widely known in the community as someone who mentors the next generation of engineers. And it's typically more fulfilling if your brand is rooted in your purpose.

TRY THIS: Take steps to develop your brand

Spend some time (start with an hour) reflecting on your brand. What is fundamental to it? How does it fit your goals? Re-evaluate your brand periodically. It can change. What do you want your brand to be? How do you want it to evolve?

Chapter 3: Summary — Vision

1. Add non-negotiable time (NN-time) to your week. Increase the time to what you can handle.
2. Make time to explore your choices. Leverage your NN-time to decide what to do and schedule extra time into your week.
3. Reflect and learn at least weekly, ideally daily. Document this quarterly or every school term.
4. Start something on the side to explore and test your skills.
5. Validate your North Star. Network with a person a day, more if possible.
6. Build self-awareness. Reflect on yourself. Get others to help you reflect.
7. Get to know your tendencies.
8. Invest in your strengths. Explore new potential strengths.
9. Find your *why*.
10. Develop your brand.

A useful way to create a vision for your future would be to spend time reflecting daily (or at least weekly) on positive stuff: what you liked, interested you, excited you, strengthened you over that period of time. Also take time to think of the negative stuff: what you didn't like, weren't interested in, didn't excite you, or weakened you. Which ones are related to your program of study? The environment you're in at school? The friends you hang out with? The other activities you do? Once you do this, create an action plan that will allow you to do more of the positive stuff. And, while you might not be able to avoid the negative stuff, you can think about ways to address it.

Vision: Resources

This resources section will contain a treasure trove of some of the content I have gathered that validated some of the realizations I had. This kind of section is normally featured in the back of a book, but I wanted to make sure that they were up front. Many resources helped validate what I understood to be true, or spoke to those truths with a clarity that made them easier to understand. I have outlined a number of topics, presenting the tip of the iceberg where these resources have delved deep under the surface. I have organized the list by individuals, organizations, or other places to get content, but this is by no means a comprehensive list of what they have produced. Choose ones that align with you and treat the content creators as mentors you've never met (although, of course, there's nothing stopping you from meeting these individuals one day). Each share similar messages in a slightly different way and using a different perspective, so find which ones resonate with you.

Books: I make it a point to read at least thirty minutes every day, although I'm not always successful. I was not always an avid reader, but now I hope to finish a book a week. Especially after learning that Bill Gates, Warren Buffett, and many successful people also read frequently. A realization I had is that books are like the movie *The Matrix*. In the movie, characters would have information downloaded into their brains from little tapes that taught them kung fu or how to fly a helicopter. While a book isn't as quick, if you think about it, the person writing the book is likely an expert in their field and probably took ten, twenty, or even more years of their experience and put it in a 300-page book. A typical adult reads anywhere from thirty to sixty pages per hour when you factor in the technical nature of learning new concepts. So, it could take you ten hours to consume ten years of information. Not too shabby! And if you're not a fan of reading, find the audio book version.

Podcasts: I do quite a bit of driving. A few podcasts along the way help minimize the road rage, so much so that I enjoy driving in traffic. But I found that my mind wandered while listening. It was actually when I increased the listening speed to 1.5× (and now 2× speed) that I was able to pay more attention. Or perhaps it was the meditation that I started which helped with my focus. Whatever the case, if you drive, take public transit, run, or engage in other activities where you can listen to something for extended periods of time, then I highly recommend subscribing to a few podcasts.

Anthony Robbins

I grew up with Tony Robbins as the infomercial guy. He had tapes available with his motivational message. However, I only started to consume his content this year and so much of it was SIWIKE! My earlier perception of him as just a motivational speaker was misplaced. He is a transformer of lives. With a background in NLP (neuro-linguistic programming), and having worked with many high-profile organizations and celebrities as well as regular folk, his messages hold a lot of value to me.

Books: *Unlimited Power: The New Science of Personal Achievement; Awaken the Giant Within: How to Take Immediate Control of Your Mental, Emotional, Physical and Financial Destiny!*

I found myself nodding my head while reading many of the chapters in these two books. I also found myself shaking my head as I asked, "Why didn't I pick up this book before?" Tony is SIWIKE embodied for me. *Awaken the Giant* is aptly named as there are concepts as well as tactical tips to help you find more of yourself and make changes for the better.

Podcast: *The Tony Robbins Podcast*
https://www.tonyrobbins.com/podcasts/

This podcast has various interviews and excerpts that share Tony Robbins' message on a variety of personal and professional development topics. There are not too many episodes as of the publication date of this book, so you should be able to catch up easily.

Gary Vaynerchuk

Although Gary Vee is known as a digital marketer and business man, he has views on self-awareness that I identify with. I started listening to Gary's podcast near the end of 2016 for his marketing content, but many of his views on self-awareness and emotional intelligence resonated with me. His content is more recent, so I couldn't have benefitted from it during university, but you can if you're still in school.

Book: *#AskGaryVee: One Entrepreneur's Take on Leadership, Social Media, and Self-Awareness*

This book is not a transcription of the podcasts. It's more of a highlight reel. There are a lot of important nuggets in there.

Podcast: *Ask Gary Vee Audio Experience*
https://www.garyvaynerchuk.com/podcast/

There are a lot of episodes, and even though most are relatively short, Gary has started creating content almost daily, so it might take you a while to catch up (though you don't have to start at the beginning).

Lewis Howes

Lewis is a pro athlete turned lifestyle entrepreneur. My interests align with his mission to help others do what they love. From an athlete, he moved to being a social media guru and now helps people on the entrepreneurial journey.

Books: I haven't yet read his books, but they are on my to-read list. I will get to them soon!

Podcast: *School of Greatness Podcast*
https://lewishowes.com/sogpodcast/

With over 500 episodes, there is a lot of content to cover.

Jim Rohn

A wealth of knowledge that could probably fit into any of the toolkit sections. I would also put him in the finance section as his views of money and its value were eye-opening for me. Jim is an author of many books that are all worthwhile reads. Unfortunately, he passed away in 2009, but he has been an influence on or a direct mentor of many of the resources I've provided, and many of their ideas are a variation of what Jim taught.

Book: *The Jim Rohn Guides Complete Set* (guides to Time Management, Personal Development, Leadership, Goal Setting, and Communication)

The guides are aptly named and provide the wisdom of Jim Rohn on the respective topics.

Stephen Covey

One of the greats in the world of personal development.

Books: *The 7 Habits of Highly Effective People* and *First Things First*

Stephen's books are considered classics in personal and professional development. There is a lot of great information to learn in them.

Carol Dweck, PhD

Carol Dweck's book *Mindset*, which originated and popularized the concept of growth mindset, solidified what I had learned and experienced by expressing its ideas in terms that were understandable and grounded in science. Her concepts are making their way into the mainstream education system.

Book: *Mindset: The New Psychology of Success*

A short read whose central concept of a growth mindset helped me solidify the concept of SIWIKE to share with others. This was definitely Stuff I Wish I Knew Earlier. Although it wouldn't have been available before 2006.

Tim Urban

Tim has a notable TED talk on procrastination and offers various college prep services. I found him through his blog, which was recommended to me.

Blog: *Wait but why*
http://waitbutwhy.com

A comical and very informative blog on a variety of topics.

I've found many of Tim's explanations of concepts helpful, and I've enjoyed reading his posts. Although some posts are quite lengthy, they are worth the time to read. A couple that stood out: one about why you should stop caring what other people think and one in the Elon Musk series about cooks and chefs — they might seem like unrelated topics, but trust me, you'll understand when you read them.

Marcus Buckingham and Strengths Finder

An author who helped pioneer the strengths revolution from the Gallup search that created the StrengthsFinder assessment tool. A friend with a crush on Marcus Buckingham suggested I read his books. I didn't. When I learned Deloitte, my current company, was collaborating with Marcus Buckingham, it made him more intriguing.

Books: *First Break All the Rules: What the World's Greatest Managers Do Differently*; *Now, Discover Your Strengths: How to Build Your Strengths and the Strengths of Every Person in Your Organization*; and *The One Thing You Need to Know ... About Great Managing, Great Leading, and Sustained Individual Success*

First Break All the Rules was probably the first book that started me on my self-reflecting journey. It started as an attempt to grow as and become a better manager. I was turned on to the concept of strengths and leveraging your strengths. I moved on to *Now, Discover Your Strengths* and *The One Thing You Need to Know*. Read these. Find out what your strengths are. The tests and assessments included can change as you reach the various epiphanies in your career.

Gretchen Rubin

I previously mentioned Gretchen in the section on tendencies and she has various helpful resources. I have only read her book *Better Than Before*, and I listen to a podcast episode here and there.

Book: *Better Than Before: Mastering the Habits of Our Everyday Lives*

I mentioned this book earlier. It can help you improve your habits. Her other books on happiness are on my to-read list, and you should check them out if that's a topic that you want to dive into.

Podcasts: *Happier with Gretchen Rubin*
gretchenrubin.com/podcast/

Her podcast provides discussion around her various books. Tendencies are revisited with additional commentary and shared experiences from listeners.

Simon Sinek

I saw a few TED talks and interviews with Simon and his focus on *why* was appealing.

Books: *Start with Why: How Great Leaders Inspire Everyone to Take Action*

For some reason, I kept delaying reading *Start with Why*, likely because I thought I already understood what Simon had to say. I did get around to reading it, and I think it is impactful when looking for purpose.

James Altucher

James is a business owner who made and lost millions of dollars several times. He is an author of several books. I have only listed the one I've read, but his others are on my to-read list. He has an honest style, and although you may not agree with all his views, you will likely appreciate his authenticity.

Book: *Choose Yourself!*

I didn't think I needed to read this book because the title seemed to speak for itself. I did get around to reading it, however, and there were a few useful nuggets of SIWIKE as well as some information that was presented in a different, entertaining way.

Podcast: *The James Altucher Show*
https://jamesaltucher.com/category/the-james-altucher-show/

In this podcast, James brings on various guests to explore a variety of topics, and James's authenticity comes out. I haven't yet caught up on all the episodes. I recommend starting with an episode with a guest that piques your interest.

Part 2: Preparation

Chapter 4: Check Your Vitals

I was a scrawny kid. In high school, I was 120 pounds on a 5-foot-9-inch frame. I could eat just about anything and I wouldn't gain a pound. Plus, I would still have the same energy level. I even went on a weight-gain regimen where I would eat three meals per day *and* have a drinkable meal supplement in between each meal. After a seven-day period, I gained a whopping one pound.

During the work week, I could survive on four hours of sleep. Taking a red-eye, sleeping until noon, then cranking out more than a full workday was fine. For those of you still in your teens or twenties, you might have the same tolerances. Don't get used to it. It doesn't last. For those older students, you know exactly what I'm talking about.

Fast-forward to now, I haven't grown in height and am thirty to forty pounds heavier (depending on the day and week), which in all honesty is probably closer to where I should be according to my doctor. If I play sports, I ache in muscles I didn't know existed. When I don't eat well, I feel horrible. When I don't sleep enough, I'm cranky. *But* I'm better than I was five years ago. That was a time when I was proud to need only four hours of sleep, though I'd often crash on the weekends. I'm older and feel better. I'm not at the same fitness level, but I now know the importance of sleeping and eating well and exercising.

A little self-care goes a long way

Imagine you're planning a road trip from Toronto, Canada, and it will take you to the west coast. You haven't yet decided where exactly you'll end up but you know you're headed west. You need to decide if you should go straight there with as few stops as possible or if you should take your time and really immerse yourself in the cities and towns along the way. Undaunted, you finish your research and learn what you can and start driving westward. Now imagine that you're doing it in a twenty-year-old car. Do you hope that the car was taken care of during its twenty-year life? Will you take care of that car during the journey across the country? Now imagine that road trip is the rest of your career and that car is your body.

In my school life, ramen noodles and macaroni and cheese were staple foods. Sugary drinks and salty snacks were common. There was a lot of deep fried and fatty (often bacon-flavoured) goodness. Unfortunately, your body has not yet evolved to handle all of that. Sure, it'll be fine for maybe the first twenty or so years. But your mileage (and lifespan) will reduce quickly if you don't take care of yourself. The length of your life is not the only thing affected; the quality is also at risk. Perhaps your lack of energy isn't you, it's how you take care of your body. Take better care of your body and your energy will increase. Which means you can get more done and make a bigger impact on the world.

In the words of Nike, "Just do it." Exercise is important, and exercise means different things to different people. Some people run ten kilometres every day. Others go to the gym three times a week. Others take strolls around the neighbourhood after dinner. Whatever it is, you'll want to get exercise over the week, ideally making some of it moderate or even vigorous activity. In any case, the best exercise is the exercise you do (better than no exercise).

You can also try to incorporate physically active habits in your routine: get off the elevator a few floors early and walk up the rest, get off a stop or two earlier when you take transit, incorporate a workout over lunch, take walking meetings. While these activities may not be vigorous, they are better than no activity.

Eating right typically starts with building the right habits. Keeping snacks out of the house and understanding the snacking impulse is helpful. (Most people don't snack because they're hungry. They're usually just bored or something else accompanies or rewards the snacking behaviour.) You can even pre-plan reactions (when your server asks you for dessert, you plan to say "no, thank you" and then follow through no matter what).

I love sleeping, and I try to get as much sleep as I can, but I found that having a purpose often kept me awake. However, you need to realize that no matter how important your purpose is, taking care of yourself so that you can carry out that purpose long-term is sometimes more important. Good habits and discipline are important for a good night's rest.

TRY THIS: Try a ten-day vitals challenge

For the next ten days, get one more hour of sleep per night than usual and be consistent with how much you sleep. If you normally sleep six hours, sleep seven. If you normally sleep seven hours, sleep eight. If it fluctuates between four and twelve, get a consistent seven to eight every night.

For the next ten days, make one of your daily meals a healthy one. You can research what healthy is for you. For me it's an abundance of vegetables (preferably the green leafy kind), with a good amount of protein (animal- or plant-based) and minimal or no amounts of processed foods (stuff that has ingredients you can't pronounce).

For the next ten days, exercise for five minutes more than you normally do every day. You could spend those five minutes, for instance, doing a combination of jumping jacks, push-ups, sit-ups, and squats. Go hard and intense (at least as much as your doctor recommends) to get your heart rate up. You might not even end up sweating by the end, which is ok. Whatever you do, do it consistently every day for each of the ten days.

Up next...

Your body is your temple. Your existence is much more challenging if the building around you is crumbling. Taking care of yourself is an outward display of your ability to take care of others. When other people see that you've taken care of yourself, they recognize that you might be able to take care of what is important to them. So, take some time to prepare a good image of who you are.

Take pride in your personal presentation

One twin takes the time to iron their clothes, dresses, and grooms themselves in a neat and tidy way. The other twin throws something on, doesn't even shower, and shows up how they are. Which one would you hire? You might not ever encounter that situation, but you might evaluate and ask, who will likely have the cleaner workstation? Who might produce higher quality work and reports? Who might be better at treating their customers well? You can't know the answers to these questions since a person's appearance may have no effect on the way they work. However, there is a likely correlation between their ability to take care of themselves and their ability to take care of customers.

I admit, I'm not the most stylish person out there. A friend on a co-op term took me shopping and helped me pick out my first suit. But I do make a bit of effort to make sure I look professional. I do so because first impressions are important, and when you look good, you feel good. When you dressed up for your prom, you weren't a different person, but you probably felt that way. Take pride in yourself and your appearance. You don't have to go overboard, but the effort is noticed.

Having a good image doesn't mean you must buy $1,000 suits and other expensive clothing. It means that you must be mindful of how your professional appearance influences the perceptions of others as it relates to your job. An average-dressed lawyer and a well-dressed lawyer probably both have the same grasp of legal procedure. However, whether consciously or subconsciously, you tend to perceive the better dressed one as the more effective lawyer (i.e., because they're able to spend more, they are probably more successful). Looking well put-together and presentable does not have to be expensive. Just be aware that your image and "playing the game" (in this case, dressing appropriately) are important. You can dress in shorts and flip-flops after you've proven yourself to be a success.

TRY THIS: Buy one set of professional clothes

As you approach graduation, the working world will present you with various professional events and occasions. I highly recommend investing in at least one set of professional clothes. You don't have to spend that much as there are many affordable options. The extra money may be worthwhile, as you're probably not growing as much as you were when you were ten, and those professional clothes may last you five years or longer. And you don't have to do it alone. Ask a friend whose style you trust and see if they can help.

Up next...

You feel good and you look good. Now let's get your mental game in order.

There's power in the present moment

My mind wanders. While I'm busy doing something, a thought pops into my head, and I suddenly realize I must do something else. Then another thought reminds me I should do another something. A few minutes pass, and I realize what I've been doing and try to remember what the original thing I wanted to be doing was. Have you ever had those moments? Working on being more present and practising mindfulness can help you avoid jumping from task to task and getting lost along the way.

I've been seeing a growing number of references to mindfulness and meditation lately. Mindfulness and meditation aren't the same thing, but they are close cousins. Mindfulness is focusing on the present. As a contrast, worrying is focusing on the past (I could have, should have, would have), and anxiety is focusing on the future (what if). If you think a little philosophically and existentially, there is nothing but the present. Well, at least until someone invents a time machine.

Meditation is an exercise in mindfulness. There are different schools of meditation. Many just get you to close your eyes and focus on your breath. Your mind wanders and you acknowledge those thoughts then focus back on your breath. To me, meditation is boring. Spending five, ten, twenty minutes doing nothing but focusing on your breath? Of course my mind is going to wander. The way I see it, that's the point. The most important part of meditation for me is the ability to refocus on my breath and on the present. Think of it like a bicep curl for focus. Meditation allows you to train yourself to be mindful. With all the distractions surrounding us today, it's growing more and more important to focus on the present.

A useful analogy is driving a car. When you focus your attention far ahead of you, not just at the hood of your car but at what you may interact with in the future, you risk not noticing that you're getting dangerously close to the car directly in front of you. The same problem occurs when you spend too much time looking in the rear-view mirror. Looking too far ahead is like anxiety. Looking at the rear-view mirror is like worry. Looking at what is around you right now is like mindfulness. Spend more time on what is around you and make sure you focus on the present, while spending a bit of time on what's behind and way in front.

Humans are also not good multi-taskers. You can only focus your attention on one thing at a time. You can do a second thing at the same time if it becomes part of your autonomous system. An example of this kind of task is driving a car from work to home. Because you've driven that route so much, it's become habitual and you're likely not to remember the trip. So, you can do one thing in your conscious mind and one thing in your subconscious mind at the same time. What people are doing when they think they're doing two things at once is task-switching very quickly. The problem is that when you switch from one task to the next, you inevitably lose things in the switch because it takes time to refocus on what you were previously doing. For some tasks, it takes fractions of a second to refocus, for others, it can take minutes. If you've ever said, "What was I doing again?" then you know what I'm referring to.

The simple solution is to have your mind be where you are. If you are at work, think about work. If you're with family or friends, be with them. If you're spending quality time with your significant other, you should put the smart phone away and not try to multi-task.

The reality is that you do have two systems that you can leverage, one that is autonomous (your subconscious) and one that is directed (your conscious). Your autonomous system has been trained by habit. It completes tasks that you have done so many times you no longer need to concentrate on them. Your directed system analyzes and makes decisions. Therefore, you can drive to work and talk on the phone at the same time, since both systems are working together. This is also why you often get to work and can't remember the drive there. And it's why the phone conversation stops when you encounter a sudden unexpected event.

But if you're on your smart phone trying to write an email while spending "quality time" with your significant other, the quality of your time will go down because you won't be giving your significant other your attention. You can get more things done if you focus on an activity, get it done, then move to the next.

Many people are busy but not necessarily productive. Although they are present, they are not present-minded, not focused on what they are doing. To be present-minded, your mind should be present in the moment. It's the opposite of multi-tasking. Being present-minded also allows you to enjoy the moment. How many times has the following happened to you? A friend is speaking to you but you're not paying attention, only listening half-heartedly while you finish writing an email. What was the question they asked? Or when you're supposed to watch your sister play a soccer game, you spend most of the game reading Facebook articles that could have waited until later in the day. How did your sister play? Did you cheer her on at all? When you split your attention, you miss out on what's happening in the now.

Being present-minded also helps your memory. Often you can't remember someone's name because you never heard it in the first place; you were thinking about something else when they introduced themselves.

Meditation can help with present-mindedness and I encourage you to take "mindful minutes" throughout the day to focus on what you are supposed to be doing. Being present-minded will allow you to be more effective in the quality of what you do, versus just the quantity of what you do. I used to be very skeptical on meditation as I didn't think I'd ever have the discipline to transcend into enlightenment. However, I found meditation to be good training for living in the present; it has helped me with focus as well as addressing procrastination. Try it and see for yourself.

TRY THIS: Practise mindfulness

Put time in your schedule to meditate. Practise mindfulness during those times. Meditate consistently for five minutes per day. Increase it to ten, then twenty, then thirty minutes.

Take some time out of your day to stop and smell the roses. Be present in the moment. Focus on one thing at a time.

Up next...

Being focused on the present comes in handy. Being able to read minds is even better. I can't teach you to do that, but you can practise putting yourself in other people's shoes to get a sense of what they might be thinking. That skill will help you immensely in your career.

Emotions have intelligence

I am pretty good at connecting with people. Well, that is, I became good at connecting with people once I started making it a priority, which didn't happen until well into my third year of university. I became better at understanding the emotions of others. When you can empathize and correctly make assumptions about what others are thinking, communication becomes much more effective, relationships improve, and you end up getting more done as a result.

The term "emotional intelligence" was popularized by Daniel Goleman, who wrote a book of the same name, although the term had appeared in earlier papers. Someone with emotional intelligence can read your emotions. They can empathize with how you're feeling in a certain situation and adapt their communication and actions accordingly. When you realize the importance of people and relationships, then you'll really understand what kind of an awesome superpower emotional intelligence is.

TRY THIS: Practise emotional intelligence

In your next conversation with a friend, spend time trying to understand how they might be feeling and what they might be thinking. Adapt your responses in the conversation accordingly. How did that conversation differ from previous conversations? Keep practising. Make it a goal to practise weekly, or daily if possible.

Up next...

You sense what people might be feeling. They might also be able to sense feelings in you. You'll want them to sense confidence, which will lead to trust and all sorts of good things down the line.

Cultivate your confidence

Early in school, I was considered smart. I was identified as a gifted student. I also did reasonably well in athletics. That gave me a lot of confidence. However, in grade five, I was bullied, which put a crack in my confidence. I buried it and tried to be outwardly confident. In high school, I was still considered smart, but I was really just living off my "gifted" status. I used that label as an excuse, thinking I didn't need to study and would just naturally be better than others. When I wasn't, I would hide behind the fact that I didn't study — I could do it if I tried. But with the cracks in my confidence, I wasn't sure. I didn't make it into the university and the program I wanted. I settled for my third choice and had to rationalize that it was the best option for me. Cracks were spiderwebbing their way through my confidence. In my first year of university, I received a letter from the administration to let me know my GPA was below expectation, and if I didn't bring it up, I would fail out of the co-op program. My confidence broke.

Then I did something radical: I tried. I studied, and I got my grades back up, but just barely. I was able to stay in my program, but I retreated inward and continued to try (this was when I started moving between classes and study carrels as I mentioned earlier). Slowly but surely, my marks went up. And as a side effect, my confidence slowly came back. I got a job in my co-op term in the first hiring cycle, which was a boost to my confidence as many only got jobs after the second or subsequent hiring cycles. The next co-op term I had a choice of jobs and my confidence continued to increase. Even after the dot-com bubble burst when many classmates with tech degrees were not getting jobs, I had a few offers. I continued to try and explore. Eventually I levelled up from my introverted nature and became an outgoing introvert. I treated everything as a learning experience, and if we fast-forward to today, my confidence is at an all-time high. It took a lot of training and cultivation to get there. You can get there too.

I like to reflect on how I was able to repair my confidence. I took an important step forward when I realized that it's okay for me to not know everything. I stopped being concerned with what other people thought of me and focused more on how I could add value to the world. Tim Urban wrote a blog post on his *Wait But Why* blog called "Taming the Mammoth: Why You Should Stop Caring What Other People Think" that articulates this journey with humorous accuracy. The blog post explains that evolution required us to care what other people thought or else we'd be kicked out of the tribe, almost certainly a death sentence at the time. But our survival instinct has not caught up to modern society where being kicked out of the tribe just gives you more time to find another tribe.

That doesn't mean you shouldn't care about what other people say. You should take the time to understand what they're saying if their comments are either accurate or relevant. If they are, then you can determine whether they matter.

Let's go through an example: You are expected to dance in front of people (something I have zero confidence doing — if I dance, I automatically think people are looking directly at me, assuming they're judging me and whispering to each other about how terrible I am at dancing — you can replace that with whatever your equivalent would be). This is when you need to pause and think about whether other people's critical comments are

- Accurate: If they say you're terrible, keep in mind that their comments are subjective. You can also ask yourself if the people judging you are qualified to judge you — if they aren't professional dance judges, why does it matter what they say? Their opinion may not even be accurate.

- Relevant: Do you have to be good at the thing you're doing? For instance, if I'm dancing, chances are I'm at a special event like a wedding. In that setting, doesn't looking funny add to the atmosphere? Probably.

After considering whether the comments are accurate or relevant, you should give yourself props for having the courage to do something you're not that great at and you're not that confident doing. Congratulations!

Confidence can be greatly influenced by the subconscious mind. It reminds me of that old parable attributed to the Cherokee where a grandfather tells his grandson that there are two wolves inside of us that are always at war with each other. One of them is a good wolf, which represents things like kindness, bravery, and love. The other is a bad wolf, which represents things like greed, hatred, and fear. The grandson stops and thinks about this for a second, then he looks up at his grandfather and asks, "Grandfather, which one wins?" The grandfather quietly replies, "The one you feed."

Although the parable speaks to good and bad, confidence and lack of confidence can also be like the two wolves in the story. If you feed your confidence by telling yourself that you can do whatever it is you want, then your mind tends to find what it's looking for. If, on the other hand, you feed the wolf without confidence, then your mind also finds the lack of confidence in you. So, feed your confidence wolf just as you would feed your good wolf.

Confidence can be practised. Getting comfortable with discomfort also helps develop a level of confidence. Another analogy for confidence is a plastic bag. If you stretch a plastic bag too quickly, the bag tears. But if you were to stretch the bag more slowly, it becomes permanently stretched and does not bounce back like a rubber band. The bag grows. So can your confidence.

TRY THIS: Build confidence

Plan to stretch your comfort level and expand your confidence on a weekly basis. Say "hi" to a stranger today. Tomorrow, engage a stranger in a ten-second dialogue. The following day, increase it to thirty seconds. Continue until you can have a full conversation with a stranger. Learn from others who are good conversationalists. Do something that is out of your comfort zone (for me it'd be something related to dancing). Do something that will make you feel awkward. Realize afterwards that nothing bad happened.

Tim Ferriss' book *Tools of Titans* has an exercise called "fear setting" where you consider the worst that could happen in a given situation. Once you've thought through the worst things, and then done whatever it is you are doing, the result is almost always better than you envisioned. You can then say to yourself "could have been worse." Ferriss suggests something as silly as lying down on the floor as you're waiting in line for coffee. Get up after ten seconds on the floor and continue waiting. You will then realize that nothing really happened. You might have gotten a few awkward looks, but a few minutes later, the awkward feeling passes. A few hours later, you don't even remember. A few days later, it won't matter.

Confidence can also be helped by gaining competence. The more you practise, the more you know, and the more confident you get. Delivering a speech on something you know very little about is daunting. Delivering a speech on something you know extremely well would be much easier.

Practise. Stop caring what others think. Be true to yourself.

Up next...

You're building your self-confidence. Your perspective and mindset can have a great impact on continued confidence. Try out a growth mindset for size. You won't be sorry.

Have a growth mindset

A Taoist parable speaks of a farmer who has the good fortune of being gifted a beautiful horse. A neighbour says, "That's good news." The farmer replies, "Good news, bad news, who can say?" A few days later, the horse runs away. A neighbour says, "That's bad news." The farmer replies, "Good news, bad news, who can say?" The horse comes back a few days later with another equally beautiful horse. A neighbour says, "That's good news." The farmer replies, "Good news, bad news, who can say?" The tale keeps going from there with the son riding the horse and breaking his leg, then not being recruited into the Emperor's army because of a broken leg and so on.

This story is an interesting illustration of mindset and perspective. Your mindset and perspective are the most important factors in reaching your potential. We've already spoken about choice, and you are aware that everything you do is a choice, and each choice has associated consequences. We've already spoken about having a growth mindset, and hopefully you are catching yourself whenever you find yourself in a fixed mindset and move towards a growth mindset. Perspective is important, and maintaining a positive perspective will allow you to achieve more.

The Secret by Rhonda Byrne discusses the law of attraction as a universal force and states that visualizing your goals will allow you to achieve them. I have been able to better rationalize this cosmic force thinking about human behaviour. My presumption is based on the phenomenon of confirmation bias: the tendency to interpret new evidence as confirmation of one's existing beliefs or theories. So, if you believe it will be true, you will find a way to make it true.

The perspective you take can sometimes will things into reality. Take the quote I live by: "I never lose. I either win or I learn." If I live by that quote, I take the perspective that I will never fail. It will be an interpretation of what happened that will make a difference to me because I will examine what I learned and will myself not to repeat the mistake. For example, you didn't fail that exam. You discovered how *not* to prepare for a test. Take those learnings and use them to improve and grow. Make the choice to change for the better.

TRY THIS: Cultivate your perspective

Reflect on the moments in your day or week where you failed or didn't do as well as you could have. How can you adjust your perspective on those moments? Combine a positive perspective with mindfulness, and practise capturing those negative thoughts in the moment and turning them into more productive thoughts that can turn into productive actions.

Up next...

You are becoming aware of your own perspective and which thoughts serve you and which ones don't. I've filled your head with a lot of knowledge so far. Wouldn't it be great if you could remember it all? Well, you can. Memory, like most things, is a skill. And with practice it can be improved. Read on to find out more!

All learning starts with memory

As a kid, I was just average at memory tasks: throughout school my memory was about the same as everyone else's. Recently, though, I've improved it and I've managed to memorize the names of thirty people around a room, most of whom I hadn't previously met. I'm definitely better at remembering names and faces than I was before.

Many people tell me they don't have a good memory. I typically respond by saying it's because their memory isn't trained. Like many skills, memory can be trained and improved. I owe the improvement in my memory to training. Memory was very important in classical civilizations before the written word was common. The Greeks specifically invented many techniques that were used to help the great orators remember all the information they had to pass down to the next generation.

BBC's Sherlock Holmes adaptation, *Sherlock,* popularized the "mind palace." In the show, Sherlock literally walks through rooms in his mind to help him remember information. Imagine remembering your grocery list by visualizing your house, walking through the front door, and seeing milk on the side table, eggs on the ottoman beside it, and bread on the shoe rack. And to recall that list, all you must do is mentally walk through your house and see those items on the pieces of furniture or parts of your house that you already know well.

A phonetic number system, which turns numbers into consonant sounds, can help you remember long strings of information. Memory-training specialist and magician Harry Lorayne popularized one version known as the major system and memory champion Dominic O'Brien has his own version he humbly calls the Dominic system. Take those consonant sounds, convert them into words, and add motion, emotion, and imagination to help your recall. There are all sorts of techniques that aid with memorization and recall that aren't taught in schools. Pick a memory system that works for you and here is a brief overview of a few memory concepts:

Linking

Humans recognize patterns and group things together. Your memories of one thing can often be triggered by another. The scent of apple pie might remind you of being at home. A certain piece of clothing might remind you of someone close to you. You can take advantage of that innate ability to help with your memory. If you have to remember a series of things, just take something that reminds you of the first item and try to imagine it alongside something that reminds you of the second item. Then link the second item with the third item, and so on. See them together as absurdly as possible. *Don't* have it make sense. Make them big, make them numerous (don't see one, see millions of them). Add motion. Add emotion and feel them interacting. Some say imagining the items with violence or with sexuality help as well (especially if you're not violent or are more conservative, as they will stand out more). Want to try? Let's see if we can memorize the Canadian prime ministers (I removed any duplicates — for example, John A. MacDonald was the first and third prime minister — to make it easier, but you can use the same techniques to add them back in.):

1. Sir John A. MacDonald: What comes to mind for me is the fast food franchise McDonald's (for MacDonald).

2. Alexander Mackenzie: When I think of Mackenzie the first thing that comes to mind is a Mack truck (like the character from Disney's *Cars*). Mack is enough to remind me of Mackenzie. If I had a McDonald's Mack truck, that would make too much sense. So to make it absurd, I would see an army of giant Chicken McNuggets (that I also try to smell) with weapons, standing in the way of the truck, looking to commandeer its contents, but the truck doesn't stop and some of the nuggets are pulverized, while others grab on to the truck as it passes and start hacking at it to get it to stop. If you don't know what a Mack truck is or have never had Chicken McNuggets, pick something that is relevant for you that relates to Mackenzie and MacDonald, but make it vivid, with lots of action or emotion.

3. John Abbott: I think of a robot (a bot). I picture Megatron, the giant robot from *Transformers,* grabbing the Mack truck and ripping it into pieces.

4. John Thompson: I imagine Thompson's WaterSeal, which is used to seal decks. I see Megatron trapped in a giant paint can and being "water sealed" in. If you don't know what Thompson's WaterSeal is, replace it with what you first think of when you think of Thompson. Perhaps Roy Thompson Hall, a famous building in Toronto, or Thomson Reuters, a large media company, or whatever is personal to you. Don't worry, with a little practice, your creativity will help you come up with future associations.

5. Mackenzie Bowell: This one is a little gross. I imagine the Thompson's WaterSeal paint can being released from my bowels. (It may help you remember if you also try to *feel* it being pushed out. If you actually felt it, it would be almost impossible NOT to remember it.)

6. Charles Tupper: I picture millions of Tupperware containers collecting what comes out of my bowels. Tupperware is a brand of storage containers and is enough to remind me of Tupper. Again, use something that is relevant for you.

7. Wilfrid Laurier: Laurier is a school close to where I live, so I picture all the Tupperware self-assembling into the school with kids playing around the Tupperware schoolyard.

8. Robert Borden: I picture Lizzie Borden, who allegedly killed her father and stepmother with an axe, hacking the Tupperware Wilfrid Laurier school to pieces.

9. Arthur Meighen: I believe it's pronounced "me-gun", so I picture myself with a gun, the biggest, craziest gun I can think of. I picture a BFG (you can look up what that stands for) from the videogame *Doom*, which was one of the first first-person shooter games made and was remade in 2016. I shoot Lizzie Borden to pieces with my crazy gun.

10. William Lyon Mackenzie King: I imagine Simba from *The Lion King* mauling the BFG gun to pieces, and "Lion King" would be enough for me to remember William Lyon Mackenzie King.

11. RB Bennett: My friend Ben skewers Simba using multiple handles of butterfly nets (Ben-net). (Of course, Ben catching Simba with the net makes more sense, but again, we're going for unexpected as it is more memorable.)

12. Louis St. Laurent: Ben suddenly drowns in the raging St. Lawrence River. The river isn't named for St. Laurent, but St. Lawrence will be good enough to remind me of St. Laurent.

13. John Diefenbaker: Diefenbaker makes me think of beef and baker, so I picture millions of steaks floating on the river and a portly baker hopping across the river on the steaks.

14. Lester B. Pearson: The baker gets run over by hundreds of airplanes, and we're now at the airport (Pearson is the international airport in Toronto).

15. Pierre Trudeau: My son attended a Saturday school class at Pierre Elliott Trudeau High School, so I picture a giant Godzilla version of my son taking his giant schoolbag and squashing all the airplanes.

16. Joe Clark: My Godzilla son gets swatted away by a giant pair of loafers (there is a shoe company called Clarks). If you don't know the brand Clarks, perhaps you picture Superman (Clark Kent) or whatever reference works for you.

17. John Turner: Someone uses a screwdriver to screw the loafers. I picture an old type of drill that requires a crank to operate — that reminds me of Turner.

18. Brian Mulroney: I have memories of Brian Mulroney and picture his giant chin chasing the screwdriver and smashing it to bits. I grew up in the Mulroney era so I have a picture of him in my head, and if you don't, use something that resonates with you. His son, Ben Mulroney, is one of the hosts of Entertainment Tonight Canada, so you could picture your local mall being destroyed by the large stone runes from Stonehenge and forming the letter E for mall-rune-E. Yes, I knew, incredibly absurd, but if you actually saw it in your mind's eye, you probably wouldn't forget it.

19. Kim Campbell: I picture Mulroney's chin being attacked by hundreds of Campbell's soup cans and eventually being put into a giant one.

20. Jean Chrétien: I picture the Campbell's soup being poured into Chrétien's iconic crooked smile. Again, Chrétien was prime minister when I was growing up so I know what he looks like, but if you don't, perhaps transform the name Chrétien to visualize a crayfish snapping their claws on your chin (cray-chin for Chrétien). Or whatever comes to mind for you.

21. Paul Martin: I had several childhood friends named Martin so they all form a gang and take turns beating up Chrétien. Since I'm not a violent person, violence would be extra memorable for me. Since you've never met my childhood Martin friends, you could picture Martin Luther King, Jr. or Martin Scorsese doing ungodly things to your crayfish chin. Or go into a local store (mart) made of aluminum (tin). Ridiculous? Yes. Memorable? Yes. If you vividly picture it, that's the important part.

22. Stephen Harper: Picture your Martin becoming sliced into pieces as he is passed through the strings of a harp.

23. Justin Trudeau: Justin Trudeau takes that harp and continually bashes it to pieces. Picture the harp being destroyed by two female deer (a doe) for two-does, which your memory should know enough to convert it to Trudeau.

Close the book after this sentence and write down as many as you can, starting with the army of McNuggets (remember to smell them). How'd you do? If you didn't get all twenty-three, then you probably didn't make the image vivid enough, big enough, or infuse it with enough action or emotion. The crazier the better. Don't necessarily use what I put, since there are some personal references in there. Use images that are meaningful (and memorable) for you. You don't remember the normal mundane events, you remember the random out-of-place events, so there's a reason this technique works.

Phonetic number system "alphabet" (major system)

This technique is useful for remembering sequences of numbers. Each number is made of consonant sounds. The numbers are turned into words. For example, the word car is made of a c/k sound, which translates into a 7, and an r sound, which translates to a 4. So, the number 74 can be represented by the word car. Vowels don't matter in the phonetic alphabet, so 74 can also be represented by the word core or cure. Now, if you combine sequences, you might only have to remember a few words or even a single concept to remember a long series. It's just as easy to remember a red car (4174), as it is to remember a car. Or a fast, red car (8014174). How could this be useful? How about remembering someone's phone number with a concept? Your social insurance number? Your credit cards? People's birthdays? The manufacturer's part number of a product? Here's the rest of the numbers and their phonetic representation if you're interested:

> 0 is represented by the sound s
>
> 1 is represented by the sound t/d
>
> 2 is represented by the sound n
>
> 3 is represented by the sound m
>
> 4 is represented by the sound r
>
> 5 is represented by the sound l
>
> 6 is represented by the sound sh/j
>
> 7 is represented by the sound c/k
>
> 8 is represented by the sound f/v
>
> 9 is represented by the sound b/p

Remembering names

I'm sure you've forgotten someone's name before. It happens to all of us. Here are a few techniques that can help you remember names:

1. Hear the name: Sometimes when you meet someone new, you are too busy thinking of what to say or are distracted by something else, and you don't actually hear the name. Make sure

you hear it. If you didn't, then ask the person to repeat it. For names you're unfamiliar with, you could ask the person to spell it for you. You could also ask if it has a meaning or how they were named to make it better stick in your head.

2. Associate the name with the face: Make a representation of the name, just as we did in the prime minister example, and associate it to a key feature of the person's face. If the person's name is Matt and Matt has a prominent nose, picture a rug (mat) slapping him across his nose causing it to be bloody. Even picture the splatter hitting you and getting on your clothes.

3. Reinforce the name: Use the person's name throughout the conversation. Continue to visualize the image.

When you see the person again, use what you visualized to remember their name! All of this forces you to put in an effort and allows you to better remember because you made observations in the first place.

With the invention of smart phones, most information is available at your fingertips, so remembering things almost seems unnecessary. When was the last time you had to remember someone's phone number or email address? The information is typically stored in your contact list. But if you recall a moment when someone unexpectedly remembered your name, or the event where you met, or what you were wearing, or what you ate, you will know how amazing and important you feel at that moment. It's as if this person feels you're so special that they remember those seemingly unimportant details. And that salesperson that knows the model names and features of every product? Don't you trust them more because it seems as if they know what they're talking about when they make recommendations? Dale Carnegie sums it up with "A person's name is to that person the sweetest, most important sound in any language." Remembering other details about that person can be a whole symphony to them.

TRY THIS: Train your memory

Invest in completing a memory course. When I was growing up, Harry Lorraine sold memory-aide tapes through infomercials. Jim Kwik trains many celebrities and executives on improving their memory. There are YouTube videos and podcasts on the subject. Most of the basic concepts are the same, so pick the one that resonates with you most. The most important part is to practise. Plan to apply the techniques at your next opportunity. Why do these techniques work? They work because they force you to pay attention, to focus and then spend time with remembering. It won't be natural at first, but like most things, practice makes permanent!

Up next...

So far, we've discussed the importance of getting your body and your mind in good shape. Now we want to turn towards your bank account. Yes, that's right, a discussion on jobs and careers will eventually turn to a discussion on money. Let's get you to improve your relationship with money.

Chapter 5: You're More Wealthy Than You Think

As this is a career-focused book, we need to talk about money. Keep in mind that I am not a financial advisor, and that you should consult your financial advisor about your specific situation. That being said, there is not a lot here that most financial advisors would contradict, as most of it is common sense and I haven't gone into many specifics.

Money can be a touchy subject for some, but managing it appropriately is a vital part of getting your career going. Ultimately it can help you find that something you are inspired to do. And if you focus on creating value, then money follows. We go through this part of the toolkit first because your financial well-being has a huge influence on the base of Maslow's hierarchy of needs: physiological needs and safety. Some of you might have had to save up and pay your own way through school, while others might have been blessed with parents who were willing and able to fund your education.

Because money is so important, it's a shame that there isn't more emphasis placed on learning to manage it. I guess it's assumed that parents will teach their kids about money, but usually those lessons come in the way they manage their money. Your parents' relationship with money will influence the relationship you have with money for your career and for your life. If your parents are frugal, you probably are too. If your parents spent a lot of time worrying about money, then you probably do too.

So if your parents weren't great with money, you likely won't be good with money, and when your relationship with money isn't good, you could face all sorts of unnecessary challenges in the future. The next sections contain some food for thought to help you maintain your financial health.

Create an abundance mindset

I was never really good with money. At least that's what I kept telling myself. I made more than many of my friends, yet somehow I couldn't keep as much of it as I wanted. Part of the challenge was that I always felt that money was scarce. I didn't have enough. I would do what Robert Kiyosaki and David Chilton prescribed, but it wasn't until I heard the message from Tony Robbins that it started to click.

The reason I didn't have enough was because I thought I didn't have enough. Your thoughts powerfully shape the world around you. Too mystical for you? Here's an example that might help, which I've pieced together from numerous sources, and it makes the most sense to me.

Have you or someone you're close to ever bought a new car, then right after you started seeing that car everywhere? You never noticed it before, but now a day doesn't go by without you seeing one. That's because you have a reticular activating system (RAS), which is responsible for taking all the stimuli around you and letting you know when there's something worth paying attention to. You had no real sense of this car before, but now that you bought one, your RAS brings it to your attention whenever you see one. Basically, your thoughts are what program your RAS. This is related to confirmation bias, which is the tendency to interpret new evidence as confirmation of your existing beliefs or theories. Confirmation bias happens largely due to the programming of our RAS. If we think about it, we'll find it. If we don't think about it, well, why would we find it?

Relate that back to money. I thought I didn't have enough money; therefore, I didn't have enough money. The simple answer is that if you feel that you have enough money, then you will always have enough money. That's what is called an abundance mindset.

When you put an emphasis on practising gratitude, your mindset changes. Being thankful lets you appreciate what you have. It allows you to focus on improvement and growth. On the other hand, if you're always focusing on what you don't have, then it could lead to jealousy and depression.

I used to compare myself with others around me quite a bit. And if I looked for it, sure enough, I'd find someone with a better phone, clothes, car, house or whatever. What I rarely considered were the millions of people who don't have a phone, clothes, car or shelter. There is only one comparison that is important and that is with yourself. Are you better today than you were yesterday? And if not, how could you make yourself better today than you were yesterday? Stopping the comparison is an important part of the abundance and gratitude mindset.

Having an abundance mindset and practising gratitude are important components of being wealthier than you ever imagined.

I don't mean that you should be content and do nothing. Instead, go out and *do something* to make your life better while thinking there's enough money, and be happy with what you have. Focus on the abundance, and your RAS will make it so. It's not easy, but it is simple.

TRY THIS: Focus on what you have, not what you want, and practise gratitude

Catch yourself in times when you compare yourself with others. Be happy for that person and what they've been able to acquire, and focus on how you could get the same and even more.

Practise gratitude. Take a minute every morning to write down three things you are thankful for — a relationship you have, an opportunity that is coming up, something you experienced in the past, or something simple you may take for granted like running water or sunshine.

Up next...

Take your new perspective on wealth and money and continue to focus on gratitude. Now let's get into some fundamentals of managing your money.

Good money management is learned, not inherited

I never thought too much about money while I was at school. My parents paid for my first year and I paid for my subsequent years from the money I earned through summer jobs and co-op terms. My parents didn't make me pay rent and I didn't have too many expenses other than tuition, books, and going out. I never considered myself rich, but I never found myself wanting for anything, so perhaps I was in a sense. One SIWIKE I found is a great definition of rich and poor, which led me to my first realization for how vital financials are. The definition is outlined by this example:

- Rich = making $1,000 per month and spending $995
- Poor = making $5,000 per month and spending $5,005

The simple point is if you spend within your means, you will always be rich, and if you spend outside your means, you will always be poor. Sometimes a simple change in mindset towards being thankful for what you have — a roof over your head, food to eat, a car, technology, or whatever you may take for granted — is all that you need. Being thankful for what you have and not focusing on what you don't have will go a long way to help your financial sanity.

This change in focus does not necessitate that you go without nice things. If you want a nice car, clothes, shoes, house, whatever it is, that's fine. But you should focus on the purpose of those material possessions. If you've always dreamed of owning a nice watch, then that's fine, but you should understand that a $200 watch tells the time just as well as a $1,000 watch. Money is important, but it's not the be-all and end-all. And society is built around getting us to spend. Marketers tell us that we need a new phone, watch, car, or whatever. And they encourage us to compare with one another, so that we can try to one-up our neighbours. Hopefully I don't stall the economy by getting people to live within their means, but something tells me the world will be just fine if you do. Sorry to be a little preachy, but moving away from material goals is an important step to having career freedom and feeling successful.

As I reflect, I guess I was rich while I was in school according to my previous definition, but I feel I could have been wealthy if I did a better job of budgeting and saving. Starting to save early is helpful. Don't put off until tomorrow what you can do today. The reason is this: compound interest. How powerful is compound interest? How about we illustrate with an example question. Would you rather have $100,000 or a penny that doubles every day for a month? It's hard to think that the penny would amount to much, but even if you pick February, with only twenty-eight days, you'd have $2.7 million. If you were smart and picked a thirty-one-day month, then you would have $21.5 million. Many financial books have other great examples, where if you started work at twenty and retired at sixty-five and contributed for first ten years of your career then stopped, you'd make more than if you contributed for ten years before you retired. Not just more, but orders of magnitude more. So, if you want to optimize your finances, then get some good resources or find a good financial advisor.

Even as a student, saving for your future is a good idea. I knew that SIWIKE but didn't put it into action. I would be much better off if I had.

One key to good money management is to know how much you make and where your money is going. Simple, right? Basically, everyone knows their salary or hourly wage. Perhaps you know how much money comes into your bank account each pay period. The challenging part is often getting a true handle on expenses.

Spending within your means typically starts with an understanding of what you make and probably more importantly, where your money is going. After taxes, benefits deductions, and whatever else is taken by the government, your employer, and whomever else, the amount of money coming in to your bank account monthly is not your salary divided by twelve. I suggest you take a weekend and do a budgeting exercise: figure out how much is coming in and how much is going out.

I am not a financial expert, so you'll want to consult with a professional, but it's a good idea to at least calculate the following things monthly:

- How much you make. Your pay stubs should help with this. If you get paid bi-weekly you might need to do some math to get to a monthly value.

- How much you spend on necessities. Tally up what you spend on things like rent or mortgage, heating, and insurance, and anything else that is spent on a recurring cycle that you need to survive. You could argue that things like your phone and internet are now needed for survival. Your Netflix account might be better classified as a want.

- How much you spend on your wants. This is sometimes called "disposable income" (or discretionary expenses) — money spent on eating out, entertainment, shopping, etc.

Now, this exercise is easy for some, and there are all sorts of guides and tools out there to help. If you don't want to do the exercise yourself then find a good financial planner. Your family and friends might be able to give you great recommendations. Otherwise, reviews online should help guide you to a good one.

Then check if what you make is less than what you spend. If it is, great! And you'll want to start saving some of that balance if you don't already. If you spend more than you make, you need to start making some choices. Examine what you should prioritize and try and understand how you perceive value. Ask yourself: Do you need those things now? How much is that worth to you? A simple question to ask yourself is "in ten years, will I remember the X I just bought?" If the answer is no, then you probably don't need it. You can still choose to buy it, but understand that you've prioritized that over other things and cut back somewhere else.

I mentioned before that I had a six-figure income, and the sad realization was that I had no money. I would try to save, but at the end of the month, there was nothing to save. An easy tactic to follow is to save first. Basically, the day your paycheque comes in, have an automated withdrawal that goes into a separate savings, investment, or other account that is harder to get at. The rationale comes from the study of human evolution: If we are in a period of abundance, we take advantage of it as we do not know if that abundance will continue or end. Similarly, if we see a large bank account balance, we tend to take that abundance as something we want to take advantage of, and we end up spending it. "Saving first" basically tricks your evolved brain into thinking that there isn't an abundance. You're not as willing to go through your minimal stockpile.

If your wage is reasonable, you can almost always live on slightly less than what you make. If you didn't see that extra money in your bank account, then you're not going to spend it. You must also have the perspective that the saved money is "off limits" and only to be touched in true emergencies.

You might be asking yourself "how much should I save?" Most experts will say about 10 percent of your income, but, really, you should save as much as you can. You should also have an emergency savings fund to give you a safety net. The recommended emergency fund is typically three to six months' worth of expenses. Why? Well, that's how long the typical job hunt takes, and having a buffer gives you peace of mind. Having an emergency fund means that if something financial unexpectedly affects you (you get fired, downsized, your company goes out of business, or you run into critical personal challenges), then you can reduce the anxiety by at least knowing that you are financially sound for a little while. It also means that your real savings don't have to be touched in emergencies and can continue to grow for your long-term.

You may live paycheque to paycheque, where your income is exactly equal to your expenses. So how could you possibly save 10 percent, let alone more than 10 percent? That's where "save more later" comes in. What is "save more later"? It's taking future earnings and committing them to savings. Here's the premise: You first start saving whatever you can and for argument's sake, let's say it's only 1 percent. Great, that's better than nothing. The year passes and you can secure a 3 percent raise of your salary. Congrats! Now here's where the "save more later" part comes in. You take that 3 percent and put it into savings. So, that initial 1 percent is now 4 percent. Get it? The simple rationale is that if you have lived on that salary in the past, then you can do so in the future. You just need to delay the gratification of being able to buy more things.

And if you don't want to fully deprive yourself, you can take half of it, say 1.5 percent, and put it to your savings and use the remaining to better your life financially. But the next year you want to take another 1 percent and add it to your automated savings. After a few years, you'll hit that 10 percent mark.

What about contributing to your emergency fund? Well, you can use the same tactics as I described above, but allocate a portion to fill up the emergency fund. Things like bonuses or tax refunds can help as well. Delay the urge to splurge and spend that bonus or tax refund, and take all of it, or at least a portion of it, and put it in that emergency fund.

As a starving student, you might only be able to save a modest amount. The point is to build those savings habits since those small percentages start adding up when you start making more in the course of your career.

TRY THIS: Get smart about your money

Start now. Set up an automatic withdrawal from your account into a savings account. Start with as much as you can manage and aim to get to at least 10 percent within a few years. Plan to take 50 percent of every future raise that you earn and add that to the savings amount.

Take time to create a budget. Block off two hours to examine what you earn versus what you spend. Refresh and reflect on your spending habits annually and plan to adjust them appropriately.

Before you make each credit purchase, reflect on whether you have the money in your bank account to pay for it. If not, consider if you can delay the purchase until you do have the funds (i.e., check to see if it is a need rather than a want).

Reflect on any negative thoughts that you "do not have enough" and prepare for the upcoming week so you can convert those thoughts into actions.

Up next...

Social media might make managing your finances more difficult. Why? Because it seems that one friend or another is always going on a nice trip or eating at a fancy restaura nt or buying a stunning new outfit or getting a new something-or-other. This makes it more tempting for you to want to go on a nice trip, eat at fancy restaurants, buy yourself a new outfit, and get yourself a new something-or-other. If you can avoid the temptation, you will set yourself up for future success. And you don't have to cut up your credit cards to do so. However, you do need to change your perspective on what a credit card should be used for.

Credit or convenience

The term credit card is accurate. The card provides you with credit from the bank that allows you to make purchases. Too many people are using credit to buy things with money they haven't yet earned. You should only purchase something on your credit card if you know you have the money to pay for it — not will have, but *do* have. This means that at the end of the month there should be a zero balance on all your credit card statements. Credit companies make enough money on transaction fees, and you don't need to help them make more.

For those that have dreams of home ownership, the ability to save several hundreds of thousands of dollars to buy a house outright doesn't seem reasonable, so taking a mortgage is an acceptable use of credit. However, buying a house that is totally beyond your means isn't reasonable. What I've read is that our mortgage payments or rent should not be more than 25 to 30 percent of your before-tax income (check a trusted source for the value that applies to you). With the ridiculousness of housing prices in many parts of the world, it seems like most of us are destined to live in a closet-sized apartment, but depending on your financial situation, you might be able to afford less or more. Consult your financial advisor for your specific situation.

Many credit card companies go on campus to try to get you to sign up with them. Some finance professionals encourage you to sign up if you are eligible as you can start building your credit early. You might not use the card but you are still building your credit history in the process. If you do use it, make sure you have the funds to pay off the balance every month. And be careful never to miss payments, or you'll end up hurting your credit score. What you want to do is to build credit to allow for more convenience in the future, not bad credit to inconvenience you later on!

TRY THIS: Review your relationship with credit

Pause before making a credit card purchase to confirm that you have the funds. Be diligent about paying off your balance. Look to maximize your rewards and benefits, balancing time and cost. Learn from others around you who have good money management skills.

Up next...

You've learned that using plastic payment for convenience is great only if you have the money in the bank and borrowing on credit is bad when your bank account can't afford it. Now, let's figure out how to pay down that balance by doing more with your interests and talents than you thought.

Profit from the side hustle

I met someone who graduated from school with a psychology degree. As she was searching for a job, she watched a YouTube video on how to make jewellery. She decided to go out to a craft store and buy all the raw materials and found out she had a knack for making it. She decided to sell the jewellery online on the Etsy marketplace, where many creative people sell their wares. She now makes more than she would be making with an entry-level job, and has found a real passion in her designs.

My story isn't as fun as that. I left my lucrative management consulting role to contract at a bank, as contractors tend to get more take-home pay than their full-time counterparts. On the side, I would go out and see who needed career coaching and what coaching they would pay for. A year later, I decided not to pursue a contract renewal, and instead I did career coaching full-time.

Earning money is great, but providing value is what's important. The funny thing is that they are one and the same thing. Follow me on this. Have you ever thought about what money is? Yes, you could say it's the paper or polymer base on which it's printed, or the digital numbers in your bank account. However, it is also a representation of value. Before there was currency, people traded. That trade might be a chicken for several loaves of bread or vegetables or furniture or something that was of value to the respective people. Money was created to help simplify that transaction of the exchange of value.

Unfortunately, the meaning of money has become removed from its original intent (highlighted by the fact that people often get paid for work regardless of how well it was done). But if you understand that fact and provide value for others, then what remains is converting that into money. Continue to provide value and that conversion should be easy.

There is a growing trend of people doing things on the side. Many started doing things as hobbies and realized that these things were valuable to people, and they could charge money for them. Someone who enjoys baking can sell cupcakes for kids' parties. Someone who loves technology can hone their skills by building websites for others. Someone who enjoys gardening might be able to help someone else landscape their backyard. And they may make a few extra bucks on the side.

I'm not saying that you have to turn your personal interest into your primary source of income, but I would encourage you to try to make some money out of it. One reason is that money represents value. If you can make a dollar then the person that bought from you values what you provided at that dollar. It can give you a good sense of how to add more value in the future. Keep in mind that some things are valued more than others, which means that turning a hobby into a primary source of income might not allow you to sustain your standard of living. But why not give it a shot? You might at least make some extra pocket money or offset the cost of a hobby you would be spending time on anyway.

TRY THIS: Make money from your hobby

Take the hobby that you were using to explore your strengths and focus on the money-making aspects. Sell one item you've created and make one dollar in profit. Increase those sales. Refine your target market to add more value, listen to your customers, and grow your hobby business.

Up next...

Now that you're starting to become healthier, wealthier, and wiser, let's move on to interacting with the outside world. Here, communication is key.

Chapter 6: Communication Is Connection

I did not do a great job at building relationships during school. There are all sorts of people I interacted with at school that have gone on to do interesting things. I was an introvert, and the thought of meeting people and networking made me cringe.

Likewise, most people cringe a little when I say they need to network. Networking brings up thoughts of small talk. Often people would rather do just about anything than stand around and talk about the weather and other seemingly meaningless topics. Most don't enjoy the small talk or the mix-and-mingles and hate the stress associated with them. To help them, I recommend they change their perception and ask them to BMC instead. BMC stands for Build Meaningful Connections, and is the exact opposite of small talk (I call it "big talk"). It's usually the reason why you and the other person are in this location in the first place. When you're at a professional event, ask another person about their interesting background. Find the SIWIKE they can share with you, and sometimes more interestingly, try and figure out the SIWIKE you can share with them. Much easier said than done, but that's the goal.

Before we discuss how to BMC, let's focus a bit on why your network is so important. For one, there is no better way to get perspective on what's out there in the marketplace than being out there yourself, be it in your industry, a related one, or a totally different one. It's much more engaging to get the perspective from someone who has experience compared with reading the reviews online, plus you get the opportunity to be exposed to other things you wouldn't have otherwise known about.

Networking meetings and informational interviews are both networking concepts, but both are unfortunately focused on the goal of getting a job. I prefer to call them curiosity conversations. The whole premise of a curiosity conversation is that a job is taken off the table, and you work instead to Build Meaningful Connections. And when you're curious about a topic, you want to reconnect in five months to find out what happened. And then re-engage every five months for the next five, ten, twenty years to get a regular update on the evolving story. Throughout this you should be figuring out the value you can provide to the person that you've built the relationship with over those months or years. Now that's a meaningful connection.

Also, when folks are in a stable job and things are going well, they tend not to think of the job hunt. But I suggest that you always leave yourself open to opportunities. Your network is the best way to help you be aware of future opportunities. In my experience, having a strong network allows for the jobs to come to you instead of you having to seek jobs. So, let's get into how to start building your network.

Now why is your network so important? Let's walk through this scenario: Let's say you oversee the process of hiring someone new to your group. There are two candidates — a random person who is qualified who submitted their resume and your best friend who is equally qualified for the role. Who do you choose? They are both equally qualified, so your best friend of course. Okay, so let's adjust the scenario and say it's the same random qualified person, but this time it's not your best friend. Instead, it's the best friend of a colleague whom you trust. Who do you pick? What if it's not a best friend but just a friend? What if it's not a friend, but someone you just occasionally hang around with who you think is a decent person? What if it's someone you met once and they seem all right? In pretty much every instance, all things being equal, you'll pick the person you know or even kind of know. However, if you're in the suboptimal scenario where all things are *not* equal, then the familiarity may still work in your favour. You might be slightly less qualified, but since I've interacted with you before, then I might still pick you. So, in any case, try to be the known person versus the random person.

Each relationship you build is like a lottery ticket, except you don't know what the odds are or what the payout might be. You might have to answer an extremely tough skill-testing question only to get a "thank you, try again." Or you might win instant millions. Or anything in-between. Now, the great part of this network lottery is that you can influence the odds and payout. If you spend time adding value to the other person, then your likelihood of a payout is much higher. Plus, the size of the payout might be greatly increased for every authentic and value-adding interaction. And if you can do so without the expectation of a payout, then the amount increases as well. If only the lottery and gaming commission had this game available…

So now that you know that networking is important, the question is, should you seek out quality (deep relationships) or quantity (a lot of relationships)? My answer is both. Relationships need to be a priority, and you need to have a variety of quality relationships along with a good quantity of relationships. That doesn't mean that every connection you make needs to be a deep relationship. With practice, you can even make a fleeting connection, where you only meet someone once for a few minutes, into a quality relationship.

The secret to quality relationships even in a short time is providing value. We talked about that friend that is always giving. Those friends that provide value to you without the expectation of anything in return are the friends that you most often want to reconnect with. So, in the same way, a professional connection should ideally also not come with an expectation.

Relationships matter as much as results

Career success is made up of two things: results and relationships. Most people focus on results — GPA, work and volunteer experience, awards, and accolades — basically, the stuff that appears on your resume. Results are important, but focusing on them too much leads to undervaluing relationships. Relationships can accelerate or even multiply the success you've had in your results. So build your results and make sure you don't forget about your relationships.

Build your results and become a practitioner

Doing well in school doesn't mean accelerating only academically. It means taking advantage of the variety of experiences you can have while at school. Participating in work-integrated learning programs is one of the more practical ways of being successful in school. You might hear them referred to as co-operative education programs, internships or experiential learning. In these programs, you learn practical experience in a real-world work environment. Work could be paid or unpaid. Work experience comes in all shapes and sizes with varying level of flexibility, structure and names.

Whatever you call them, both are essentially work experience while you are at school in an area of industry that is related to your program of study or the direction you want to take after graduation. Not to negate the value of the typical part-time retail or service jobs that students often have during school, but internships add value as they offer direct experience in their field instead of just transferrable skill sets. I was lucky to have friends and family members convince me of the value of work experience in my field. I had the opportunity to pursue a degree that didn't have a co-op program in a supposedly better rated school but chose the school with the co-op program instead.

Once you finish school, having experience is important. Hiring companies compare their applicants, and if you have someone with work experience and someone without, all things being equal, you'd take the person with work experience. When I hire students, I'd take someone with a B average who has demonstrated work experience showing some initiative and drive over a student who achieved an A+ who hasn't done anything outside of their studies.

Learning your trade in an academic context is better than nothing, but being a *practitioner* clearly shows that you know how to do the job. You can become a *practitioner* through work experience or other means.

Work experience is a better predictor of performance than school. And sometimes the type of work does not matter (some work experience is better than no work experience). For instance, having a job in retail or fast food shows that you can get to work on time and do what you are taught. Formal co-op programs and internships help provide support to students, allowing them to get the work experience they need. And for students who aren't in those programs, I recommend working over the summer instead of taking the summer off for as many summers as you can manage.

You may end up securing a work placement for which you are tasked with only administrative activities. How could that benefit you? Surely, making photocopies, formatting documents, organizing resources, or completing other seemingly low-value tasks wouldn't be useful on your resume. Or would it? Well, what if, being in the work environment every day, you looked at the processes going on around you and read the information to understand what was being done and why it was important to the client? At the very least, you'll better understand how it all works so that for your next placement you can get started without the training time. And what if, as you are doing this routine work, you found a way to do it 0.1 percent faster than the day before, perhaps by streamlining where supplies were placed or batching copies together so you need to make fewer trips or whatever you can imagine. Over a four-month period, you might improve the overall process by 8 percent. Not too shabby at all. Now, what if you took the extra time you saved and spent it improving a related process. That might set you up for success in a future job. And I'm sure the person you are helping will be thankful for the help (think BMC). And if you spent the time to help improve that process, then all sorts of career options might start presenting themselves in the future.

You could also be a *practitioner* by sharing your knowledge and experience through a blog or some sort of periodical, by helping at an industry conference, or volunteering for an organization in a role where you can practise your skills and demonstrate your abilities. If you can't get exactly the job you want, get as close to the job as you can manage. For instance, if you want accounting experience and there are no openings in the accounting department of the volunteer organization, then handling money for a fundraiser, making sure that everything is accounted for and balanced, would be the next best thing.

One important part of getting this experience (whether it's paid or not, supported by others, or initiated by others), is to turn the work into an achievement. Don't just do the work to be able to say that you did it, do it so you can say *how well* you did it. Look at the Job Hunt section in Chapter 9 for the difference between activities and achievements to understand why.

The other side effect of getting the experience is to confirm that what you're doing is what you want to be doing. Why wait until you get your full-time job to verify if you like what you've been studying for so many years? Research these opportunities to get a better sense of what options are out there. Starting early exposes you to the possibilities and can open your eyes to opportunities that you might not have otherwise considered. So be a *practitioner* to demonstrate you can do it and to experience for yourself that you want to be doing it.

Every encounter can be meaningful

Everyone knows they need to network; however, many people don't know how. I attribute part of the challenge to the seeming death of the art of conversation. I suppose it's not dead per se, but the traditional romantic sense of what a conversation should be — a face-to-face, meaningful interaction — may be something of the past. Although we are more connected as a society, because many conversations take place over text or other message platforms, our interactions with each other tend to be superficial and our social media posts are easily curated to include only the best of ourselves. But what about everything that makes us who we are? Finding out all that information about each other starts by having a proper conversation. There is no substitute for a face-to-face interaction when you Build Meaningful Connections.

If you're an introvert, you might have reservations around having to BMC and all it entails. However, even as an introvert, you have it in you to make these connections. Give yourself a shot, and don't give up easily. You can't expect yourself to BMC like a pro right off the bat.

To BMC, you have to start at the end and work backwards. Start with the C (Connections), then work at making the connections Meaningful, then Build them further. You first need to start that conversation or send that initial message. That can be a daunting task, but again, with practice, you can get over the fear of building those connections.

> After the thrill of meeting people during frosh week at university wore off, I reverted to my introverted tendencies. It wasn't until my third year that I tried to make the connection I described in Chapter 2 (the terribly awkward one from one study carrel to the next) and oh my goodness, yes, it was awkward the first time, but I soon improved. It took a long time to get to a point where I was perceived as an extrovert. However, if you see me at a networking event, my faux extroversion abounds, but by the end of the evening, I'm exhausted and you can often find me in a corner letting out a sigh, working on summoning the strength to have one last conversation.
>
> I've discovered that approaching conversations with the intention to mentor the other person or help them in some way is a useful way to leverage my strengths, and it has helped me gain energy and make the conversations much more meaningful.

Unfortunately, it doesn't stop at making the connection. Connections become Meaningful when you're able to relate to the person you're connecting with and provide value to them. And relationships become increasingly Meaningful when you Build them (by following up with the person and keeping them top of mind as you reconnect). Meaningful Connections can act as a multiplier for your career achievements.

Make Connections

Networking starts by making connections: meeting people, introducing yourself, sharing stories. I've often encountered the assumption that professional connections must happen at a networking event. Why? Why can't you connect with the person sitting next to you on the bus or train or plane? The person waiting in line with you? The person in the elevator? Or any other random stranger? Some say, "Because it's hard and I'm not good at it." That may be true. But you'll likely not improve much at making connections if you're only attempting it once a month when you attend a networking event.

The first time I made a purposeful decision to speak to a stranger, it was nerve-racking for sure. What if they don't respond? What if they think I'm weird? What if they think I'm awkward? The "what if they think" game went on for a while, until … I finally said something.

"Hi, that's an interesting bag that you have, would you mind if I asked where you got it?"

The stranger looked me in the eyes — probably taken aback a little by the interruption — and after a brief pause said, "Oh, I got it on a trip I took last year."

"Oh, that's good," was my response, followed by awkward silence. "Well this is my stop. Bye."

"Bye."

Well, that didn't go that well. And afterward I didn't beat myself up with thoughts like *Oh man! I should have said more, there was so much awkward silence*, or take on the mountain of other criticism I could have made; instead, I started with, *Wow, I'm so amazed that I did it.* Then I focused on what I learned and what I could do differently next time.

The question is, would you rather sound like a newbie when trying to make a connection with someone that could potentially be important to your future career, or would you rather have learned how to make a connection by doing it many times before? That first interaction will likely be a little (or a lot) awkward, but after you go through it, you can look back on it and see that the awkwardness or anxiety you felt really wasn't that bad. Once you've done it, it will be over (yay!) and you can work on figuring out how to make the next interaction just a little better. And the next will be a little better — and easier — still. And so on.

Make it Meaningful

Okay, so you're starting down the path to make connections with tens, maybe hundreds, more people than normal. Are those people part of your network? Yes and no. Yes, from the perspective that anyone you've ever interacted with is in your network. And no from the perspective that some interactions are better than others. How do you make that conversation better/more meaningful? It often starts by being more interested in the person you're talking to than trying to be interesting to them. Being curious about someone shows that you care, and asking them questions will allow them to discuss almost everyone's favourite subject: themselves!

Meaning can also come from shared experiences. These don't have to be the exact same experiences, but you could find commonality in places you've visited, a school you attended, foods you've tried, people you've met, topics that interest you, or your hobbies. When you find these connection points, the conversation will flow much better.

Most people I know have a button — that topic they can discuss for hours. Even the most introverted person will have something they are passionate about and excited to discuss. Once you find someone's button and you push it, you will become the most interesting person to them, just because you are interested.

And like connections, making conversations meaningful takes practice. I am not a master conversationalist, but I have improved. I still encounter awkward pauses and have conversations that are only so-so. The important thing is that I am always learning and improving. But I do stumble occasionally. So, don't worry about it. Keep at it to learn to make meaningful connections.

Build by giving and maybe, just maybe, you shall receive

Some people think that you must feel a real connection after having a conversation, that sparks will fly and it will feel like they've known each other forever, and that it's harder to stop the conversation than it was to start it.

When you BMC, it is so important to offer and give your help. When you connect with someone who could be a potential mentor or who has some SIWIKE to share, you are already taking their time. Ideally, you'd be able to return the favour. You might think that when you are early in your career, you won't have a lot to offer, but that's not true. You have more to offer than you give yourself credit for. If you've graduated, you could provide insight to post-secondary students. Post-secondary students could share their SIWIKE with high school students, and high school students with elementary school students. Also, age may not necessarily be a factor. A young person who has done something for a significant portion of their life may have more experience and expertise than someone who is older and has just started.

So now that you know you have something to offer, give it. When you BMC with someone, always offer help and add value. If you're being mentored by someone, for instance, you could offer to spread the word among your peers about the company your mentor works for. If your mentor works for a charity, you could offer to help organize parts of their fundraising event. Be creative and try to offer something.

Giving unconditionally builds a positive reputation. You become that person who is always willing to lend a helping hand. Who wouldn't want to hire that person? You get to choose which version of yourself you want to be. If you have been more of a taker in the past, the only way to shift into being a giver is to start giving once, then giving again, and so on. And if you take once in a while, that's fine too, but the more the balance lands on the giving side, the more you'll find people will be open to building relationships with you.

Social interactions follow unwritten rules

There are some unwritten rules when you BMC and for networking in general. These might seem apparent, but you'd be surprised how many people break them.

1. You should pay: If you asked them for their time, you should be the one buying. This means you always at least attempt to pay for coffee, lunch, and drinks. They may offer to pay, but you should still insist and take the initiative to pay.

2. Do what's convenient (for them, not you): Where possible you should look to make the meeting convenient for the person you're connecting with. They will be much more open to connect when the location, date, and time works well for them.

3. Prepare and be mindful of time: Take some time to come up with the questions you want to ask them. Also, be mindful of their time. If you say it'll only be thirty minutes, make sure you have an alarm or something to alert you a few minutes before your allotted time ends that lets you know that your time is up. If you can, think of ways where you could help and add value to them, and let them know before the conversation is done.

4. Listen: Some of the advice given might not be what you want to hear, but make sure you're listening since that might be the advice that you need. Don't be argumentative if you don't agree with a point they are trying to make. Try to understand their point and see what you might be missing. Also, as they are speaking, try to make connections with what you've done and see if you can offer help or lend your expertise.

5. Thank them: I have had people take up a lot of my time without a thank you. Do not be one of them. Make sure you express that gratitude. Thank the person for their time, for any advice they've given, for making (or offering to make) connections for you. Thank them before they meet with you, thank them in person, follow up with them and thank them again.

6. Remember you are not entitled: Understand that everyone has a right to say no. You are not entitled to a person's time. Don't take it personally. Reflect on how you can bring value to them, then try again. Be persistent, but understand when your time would be better spent elsewhere.

TRY THIS: Build Meaningful Connections

Make connection goals. Just like you might have goals to exercise three days per week, make goals to connect with three people per day or per week. Connect with new people. This could be strategic or random. You could even reconnect with previous contacts. Exercise your conversation muscle.

Make those connections meaningful. Practise adding value to your network. Give first without the expectation of receiving.

Next, build those connections. Create reminders to reconnect in three to nine months.

Up next...

Build Meaningful Connections and expand the relationships in your network. Note that people are different. Understanding those differences will go a long way to strengthening those relationships.

Adapt your communication style

Coming to understand the mechanics of relating to people helped me get better at making connections. When I used to explain things to people and I'd get blank stares, I would often think to myself, *Why doesn't that person get it? It's so obvious.* Learning that people communicate differently was eye-opening.

There are many models that describe communication style and personality types. They have their various uses and benefits.

The Myers–Briggs Type Indicator is common in North America, but it is limited in its use. To understand another person's personality type, the other person would have to share their test results with you. And how awkward would it be to start a conversation with "Hi, what MB profile do you have?"

Models like DISC are beneficial because they focus on what is observable. In a few minutes, you can learn to pinpoint someone's styles. I like DISC because it's one of the simpler models to understand. There are many other models out there, but the main point is to understand that communication differences exist.

Adapting your communication style based on the personality of the person you are interacting with will go a long way to help you become more effective at communicating with them regardless of the model you use. However, you need to make sure to continually reassess the person while you interact. Just because you initially label someone a D (dominant), for instance, doesn't mean you should assume this is all you need to know about them. A label will never capture the many subtleties and unique qualities that make people who they are. Make the effort to get to know each person better. Styles can be context-specific as well, so use your initial assessment as a data point based on your interaction, but don't assume it applies in all situations. Also, note that people can change their behaviour over time and learn to adapt, although it's generally accepted that people have a default for any of these styles.

Communication Behaviours – DISC

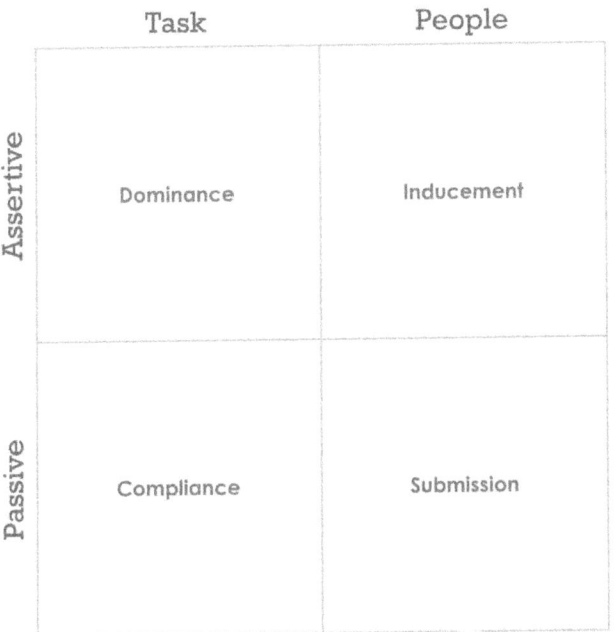

Figure 5: Sample of understanding communication styles using DISC[4]

For illustration on style variations, here's a bit of an overview of DISC. DISC puts communication tendencies in one of four quadrants.

- Assertive and task oriented: Dominance — people with this style are direct, decisive, demanding, want direction, and are doers and drivers.

---

[4] There are many versions of the DISC quadrants. I've used the original ones from William Marston in this visualization.

- Assertive and people focused: Inducement — people with this style are influential, impulsive, impressive, inspiring, interesting, and love to interact.

- Passive and task oriented: Compliance — people with this style are conscientious, cautious, compliant, concerned, calculating, careful, contemplative, and want to be correct.

- Passive and people focused: Submission — people with this style are steady, stable, sympathetic, supportive, shy, specialists, and like the status quo.

The styles are important since people in different quadrants are more likely to clash and meet in disagreement, and the categorization helps to shift the focus from who's right and who's wrong to "why do we disagree?"

DISC is just a tool to help us communicate more effectively. There are many types of assessments available. For instance, the Enneagram model discusses nine personality types; various models separate personalities and communication styles into colours; the OCEAN or CANOE model discusses the big five personality traits; and cultural diversity models help explain personality traits by being aware of and acknowledging our differences. The point is to understand that you might be able to communicate more effectively using different approaches with different kinds of people.

Many people have learned to switch communication styles to suit different people and situations. So while the categorizations can be useful, it's important to avoid sticking labels on people (including yourself). These tools can help you open the doors to effective communication before you get to know people better.

TRY THIS: Enroll in a communications improvement event or activity

Join Toastmasters, try improv, or connect with other public speaking or communications organizations. These organizations will help you improve your communication skills and make you feel more comfortable in social situations.

Up next...

Knowing that people communicate differently sets the stage for getting your intended message across. You'll come to understand that it's not only important that you understand the message, but that the person you're talking to also understands the message.

It's better to be understood than heard

Often when people communicate, they are looking to be heard. They want to impart their wisdom or even dictate their orders. When we aren't understood, we tend to just repeat the same messages louder and more intensely. But if we take the time to understand the other person's perspective and make it a goal to communicate in a way that helps them understand, then communication would be more effective. You can use yourself as a proxy. Ask what sort of communication you'd want to receive from someone and then set similar expectations with the people you communicate with. Also, be emotionally aware of the messages you send out. Emotional intelligence can be learned.

You communicate more effectively when you are clear and concise. Being clear and concise in your communication requires practice. Depending on your personality, you could be a very "to the point" communicator or a roundabout communicator.

Understand that people have their preferences in communication style, and knowing a person's preference rather than just using yours will help make communication more effective. You might have to test the waters (and maybe get it wrong at the beginning), or you can simply ask for specific feedback, and doing so will help make your communication more effective. One of the most effective ways to improve communication is to ask a trusted team member or manager to give you feedback on a presentation or a meeting you led. Let them know what you are working on and ask them to observe and tell you their perception of the interaction or presentation — not just on content you shared, but also whether the delivery was clear, concise, confident, and understood. Listen with an open mind, and thank them for helping you improve.

If you believe you are providing enough information to your manager or supervisor, try to do a little bit more. The other person will let you know if it's too much. And you can always ask to make sure there is enough communication. You'll also want to make sure the communication method is chosen appropriately as well. Some people prefer to talk "live" — in person, on the phone, over Skype — so they can ask clarifying questions and get immediate answers. Some people like to have time to review the information on their own time and at their own pace and may prefer email or text. Keep in mind that each communication method has pros and cons given the purpose of the communication and the audience.

You need to make sure you're building an appropriate relationship with your audience. Understanding the communication tendencies of others will allow for you to communicate more effectively and be better understood.

TRY THIS: Be clear and concise in all your communications

Focus on your audience. Communicate for the listener and help them understand. Exercise your emotional intelligence. Practise being clearer and more concise. Communicate more. Build Meaningful Connections.

Spend one hour reviewing your communications for the week and identify at least one opportunity where you could have

- Done a better job at keeping the audience in mind (including gaining a better understanding of communication preferences).
- Been clearer (fewer back and forths / misunderstandings) or more concise (less unnecessary information in emails / meetings).
- Communicated more.

Up next...

Adapting your communication style to be better understood by your audience is important. Another way to build a relationship is to make it less about you and more about them. Being interested in someone instead of interesting to them can be key when you try to Build Meaningful Connections.

Don't just be interesting; be interested

I've already mentioned a person's topic button — that interest the person has that makes their eyes light up. If you find it and that topic *is* interesting to you, the relationship almost can't help but become meaningful. If the topic is *not* interesting to you, you have a few choices:

1. Listen with the hopes of becoming interested — this is quite challenging.
2. Stop the conversation — this will likely prevent the connection from becoming meaningful.
3. Steer the conversation to a topic that might be more interesting — this will take some skill to master, and beware of turning to a topic that is interesting for you but not for the other person.
4. Relate the topic to something you're interested in — a win-win where you are both interested.

TRY THIS: Practise finding what is interesting

Practise conversations. Find a topic that interests the other person during the conversation. Find out why they are so interested. What part of the topic would interest you enough to find out more?

Up next...

You're now armed with many tools and foundational skills. You're mastering self-care: you're sorting out your finances, sleeping properly, eating healthy, and exercising. Let's continue to build you up and unlock your career potential.

Chapter 7: Summary — Preparation

1. Take care of your body — get enough sleep, exercise, and eat healthy.
2. Dress to impress.
3. Practise mindfulness.
4. Practise emotional intelligence and empathy.
5. Build your confidence.
6. Cultivate your mindset.
7. Train your memory.
8. Practise gratitude.
9. Manage your earning and spending.
10. Turn your credit into convenience.
11. Turn your hobby into money.
12. Build Meaningful Connections.
13. Practise communicating.
14. Show interest in others.

Making sure your physical and emotional health are sound will help make the more challenging task of finding your purpose much easier. Prioritize your well-being and get ready to explore the world and make an impact!

Preparation: Resources

Anthony Robbins

I've mentioned Tony previously, and he also has insights on finance.

Books: *Money: Master the Game*

This book helped me understand future financial planning. More importantly, its perspective on your relationship with money has made an impact on me, and it optimizes techniques from other books. The book is US focused, so take a look at David Chilton and *The Wealthy Barber* series for Canadian guidance.

David Chilton

You may know him as one of the Dragons on the *Dragons' Den* television show where entrepreneurs pitch their start-up ideas. To me, he is the Wealthy Barber.

Books: *The Wealthy Barber* and *The Wealthy Barber Returns*

These books are foundational and provide Canadian-focused financial guidance.

Napoleon Hill

Like Tony Robbins, Napoleon Hill interviewed many financial juggernauts, only he took twenty-five years to publish his findings (in 1937).

Books: *Think and Grow Rich*

This is not really a personal finance book. It's more of a personal development book focused on psychology with the end goal of increasing your financial earnings. The book has a lot of interesting insights on the psychology of money and was likely one of the sources from which *The Secret* drew its inspiration.

Planet Money

A podcast produced by NPR (National Public Radio — a public station in the US), *Planet Money* is not necessarily focused on personal finance, but it does provide some interesting and enlightening thoughts on all things finance-related. I find the information entertaining and interesting to listen to, and perhaps you will too.

Tim Ferriss

Tim Ferriss is a wealth of knowledge when it comes to learning. Tim interviews experts and finds the best way to learn to do almost anything. His content is more recent, so it would not have been SIWIKE I could have shared with my soon-to-be-grad self, but it could be SIWIKE for you. I have heard him referred to as a human guinea pig. He experiments on himself, trying to find ways to get better. He has several books, and one, the *4-Hour Chef*, introduces the concept of meta learning, which will help you learn to learn just about anything.

Book: *Tools of Titans*

This book is broken down into three sections: Healthy, Wealthy, and Wise. Some of what he discusses on health are well beyond my understanding as he is deep into the Quantified Self movement (measuring anything and everything about you — from heart rate to ketone levels, which I still don't understand — to assure optimal living). Take what makes sense to you, as there are quite a few useful nuggets.

Podcast: *The Tim Ferriss Show*
https://tim.blog/podcast/

Tim Ferriss interviews various guests, trying to reverse-engineer their success to see what could be implemented into his own life. I enjoy his interviewing style. There are upwards of 250 episodes that are about an hour each, so there's lots to consume (I don't think I'm even halfway through yet, probably because I have many other podcasts I listen to as well).

Part 3: Skill Building

Chapter 8: Motivation and Productivity Hacks

Motivation fuels your success; procrastination is the enemy

Motivation to me is wanting to do something. That motivation could be out of obligation, or from an internal burning desire to do something. Now to me, the opposite of motivation is procrastination. And I outline the relationship using this formula:

$$\text{Procrastination} = \text{Excuses} > \text{Purpose}$$

$$\text{Motivation} = \text{Purpose} > \text{Excuses}$$

I am just as guilty of making excuses as everyone else, and when I do, procrastination easily takes hold. If we can get rid of the excuses, or at least make them small enough, then motivation can replace procrastination. You can also help motivation beat out procrastination by having a significant enough purpose. If your purpose is strong, the excuses won't matter. That's what we mean when we say someone has drive: they have passion despite whatever gets in the way (like any sort of excuse), and they plow their way through a task or they find another way to get it done.

Here's an example:

I tell you that you need to spend one hour a day working on improving yourself in one of your strength areas — above and beyond what you do for school and any other work you might have — for the rest of your life.

The first thoughts that might pop in your head are: *That's so much work. How do I find an extra hour every day when I barely have enough time to do what I'm doing right now? I don't sleep enough, I don't spend enough time with my friends, I don't ... blah blah...*

Now I change things slightly and tell you that you need to spend one hour a day working on improving yourself in one of your strength areas — above and beyond what you do for school and any other work you might have — for the rest of your life, *and if you do*, I have it in my power to ensure that you will have a job with a competitive salary when you graduate that you can turn into something that provides you with purpose and fulfillment while allowing you to achieve your future hopes and dreams.

Does your purpose and your motivation change? You've heard a similar example in a previous chapter and hopefully a bit of repetition in a different context might help it to sink in better.

TRY THIS: Turn excuses into purpose

Reflect on the times during the past week when you made excuses to avoid doing something. Change the perspective of those excuses into purpose. Replace "I have to," with "I get to." Catch yourself in the moment you're making excuses. Transform the perspective of those excuses into purpose.

Your results are determined by your expectations

First, you must understand what your expectations are. How achievable, relevant, and important are those expectations? Are there more fundamental expectations that are needs and not wants? Many people face the challenge of not knowing what they want. And if they do know what they want, they don't often know why they want it. At the end of the day, what most people want is to meet or exceed someone's expectations. Who that someone is depends on the individual. You may be trying to meet the expectations of any of the following people:

- Yourself: This one is relatively easy since you're in full control; you must figure out where you got those expectations and you may need an exercise in self-awareness to adjust or realign your own expectations as appropriate.

- Your parents: This one can be quite tough as parents may want their kids to become something aligned with their own definition of success. Realigning their expectations can be challenging, but from my experience, parents just want to know that their kids are securely employed, able to give them grandkids, and are happy. Having hard discussions and having transparent communication with parents on goals tends to be a great way to realign expectations.

- Your significant other or spouse: Depending on who you pick, this could be easier or tougher than your parents. Communicate your goals, and perhaps they could even help. Make sure their needs are addressed in the conversation. Again, transparent communication is typically key.

- Your children or future children: We all want the best for the little ones that we brought into the world. Depending on your parenting and their upbringing, most children are supportive of their parents if expectations are properly set and their needs are met.

- Other relationships: This could be friends, co-workers or other people you interact with. It's possible letting them down may be just as difficult as letting down blood relatives. However, you have greater control of the friends you keep, so if setting expectations doesn't work, then new friends can be an option as well. The same thing applies to work. If you're not meeting expectations at work, you can always change where you show up and clock in every day.

- Society: This is often the most abstract concept as most people cannot imagine the scale of their impact on the world and all of society. You often generalize society's expectations for you based on what messages are marketed to you, those things you hear most often from people around you or the media. If you can manage those expectations, then you are bound for success.

Most of these are much easier said than done, and you'll have to prioritize their importance versus your own needs. At the end of the day, knowing that you have an option to define success on your own terms can be very empowering.

TRY THIS: Reflect when results don't meet expectations

Spend time reflecting on times that didn't meet expectations the past week. What did you learn? How can you make future expectations more accurate? Adjust on future expectations.

You are in control of your habits

When discussing motivation and prioritization, the topic of willpower often comes up. Much of the research available points to the fact that willpower is a finite resource that replenishes after you go to bed (and to a degree, after you eat).

Based on that fact, our willpower is highest in the morning, and doing things first thing (no matter how daunting) will allow us to take advantage of when our willpower is the greatest. Additionally, it means that our willpower is tested much more at the end of the day than at the beginning. On the flip side, it's about knowing yourself, so if you're a night owl and find that you have a renewed source of energy in the evenings, then perhaps your willpower becomes recharged then. Find what works for you.

Additionally, willpower is depleted when making decisions. Building good habits is often an important way of overcoming tests to your willpower. Gandhi said, "Your habits become your values. Your values become your destiny." That becomes quite challenging when you realize that you have good and bad habits alike. Changing behaviours goes through four stages, which I'll outline below.

When you first become aware of a habit, you can begin to change it. Let's take procrastination, something that many people tell me they struggle with. Sometimes you might realize you are procrastinating, but often you can only recognize that you *were* procrastinating after the fact. Charles Duhigg in *The Power of Habit* outlines three parts of the habit cycle you should recognize: the cue, the routine, and the reward. Recognizing the cue gets you to the state of conscious-incompetence, which is when you realize you are doing something that is not productive or aligned with your intention. You need to hijack the action that typically follows the cue to get into another action path. Sometimes you become aware that you are undertaking the unproductive action and must reset to take the alternate action path. Identifying the cue earlier on can eventually help you replace that habit with a more beneficial habit. Crafting an alternative to the action, then applying a sufficiently appropriate reward, will help you change your habits.

Here's an example: I had a class on Wednesdays in which I would sit in the back of the class. The professor had a monotone voice that for some reason was especially soothing to me and caused me to nod off. The class was after lunch, which didn't help as my full belly would make me drowsy. I would often wake up as class was being dismissed, which is not the best recipe for successful studies.

For this habit, the cue was "Wednesday and sit in the back of the class." The action was "nodding off." The reward was "a restful nap." Knowing that it was a bad habit was the first step. This can be the hardest part. The next step was figuring out how I could change the behaviour. I couldn't change the date or time of the class, so I hijacked parts between the cue and the action. I adjusted the cue by moving to the front of the class and sitting with a friend who was asked a lot of questions. The action became taking notes so as not to allow the professor to readily see me nodding off. Also, my friend and I would compare notes after class, and he would be upset if they weren't similar, and I didn't want to let him down. The reward was a slightly happier prof, a happy friend, and better marks.

Another helpful way to get things done and improve your habits is to understand your tendencies. As we discussed in Chapter 2, Gretchen Rubin introduces the concept of the four tendencies in her book *Better Than Before*, to help build in more likelihood for success. You can see from the example above that I am an Obliger and needed the double accountability of having the prof right in front of me and a friend to help support me.

Here are a few more details on working with your tendency to support habit development:

- Obligers (largest portion of the population) meet external accountability but do not readily meet goals when they set them for themselves.
    - One tactic for Obligers is to have someone help them achieve their goals. Find a workout buddy to go to the gym with. Make study dates. Ask others to follow up with you. Tell them what you are doing.

- Questioners (next large portion of the population) meet internal accountability, and do so when they have an appropriate reason. If external forces are pushing a Questioner to meet a goal, the Questioner won't necessarily do it unless they feel there is a valid reason.
    - One tactic for Questioners is to get to the why. If you are trying to get a Questioner to do something, make sure you tell them why. If you are a Questioner and need to complete a task, look for a reason to validate its completion.

- Upholders (a small part of the population) meet both internal and external commitments alike. They just get stuff done.

- - Upholders don't need much help to get motivated. They're great role models, though, and useful if you need help with something, including motivation. If you are an Upholder, congratulations.
- Rebels (a small part of the population) don't respond to either internal or external accountabilities. They just do what they want when they want, and pressing them often doesn't help.
  - Be aware of the tendency and understand that if you're expecting a Rebel to get something done, you might have to wait until they're ready. If you're a Rebel, it's hard for you to rationalize anything with yourself; however, a strong enough "why" helps pretty much all tendencies, so if you've got a good reason to do something, you probably will. Otherwise, just give yourself enough slack time to get into the mood to do something and look to make that task or the next step in that task as easy as possible to avoid the rebel from coming out in the first place.

Knowing your tendency can help you build plans and habits for you to achieve more.

Habits take time to form and develop. Research says it takes sixty-six days on average to make something stick — that's three months if you're not counting weekends, and it will be longer if it's not something you do every day. So, starting as early as you can will allow you to create great habits for the prime of your career. As mentioned above, the most typical bad habit that plagues students is procrastination. Tim Urban has an excellent and humorous post on his blog *Wait But Why* about his views on procrastination involving the characters in your brain: the Rational Decision-Maker, your Instant Gratification Monkey, and your Panic Monster. To paraphrase, evolution has provided us a capacity to think rationally, here represented by the Rational Decision-Maker, which helps to consciously steer our lives. The more primitive part of us is embodied by the Instant Gratification Monkey. The Rational Decision-Maker tries to get us to do things, but unfortunately the Instant Gratification Monkey often gets in the way, tending us towards procrastination. On occasion (typically at deadlines), the Panic Monster comes out and scares the Instant Gratification Monkey away to allow the Rational Decision-Maker to do its thing (e.g., cram).

Some people have small monkeys that get in the way only some of the time, and some people have huge gorillas (yes, yes, gorillas are apes, not monkeys, but we're talking about a monkey in your head so no need to get technical). And people can have monkeys that mutate in different circumstances; for example, when they're at work, their monkey might be well under control, but for personal matters, it becomes an 800-pound gorilla.

So, what can you do about it? In the Instant Gratification Monkey analogy, the goal is to tame the monkey. The first step here is to be aware of when your monkey is in control. According to the four stages of competence learning model which is from Gordon Training International, and which is often attributed to Abraham Maslow:

1. You start off first in unconscious-incompetence (that is, you don't know you're doing something). You cannot stop procrastinating because you do not realize you're doing it in the first place. You first must become aware that you are procrastinating. Some simple tricks to do this are to place visual cues around you, like a sticky note that says, "Are you working or procrastinating?"

2. Once you realize you're procrastinating, you've entered the next stage, conscious-incompetence (as in, you now know you're doing something stupid). At first, you won't be able to help it, but getting to the conscious-competence is the toughest part. One technique to block the bad tendency is to use if-then conditioning, which basically replaces one behaviour with another.

   For example, I wanted to reduce the time I spent on social media sites as I found that pre-rolls and autoplay just made it too easy to go from one video or article to the next. So, I spent some time thinking through what I would do instead of spending time on social media. If I became conscious that I was browsing Facebook, then I'd ask myself what I should be doing instead, and go do it. For a while, I would have to repeat the Nike slogan ("Just do it") a few times before actually getting to work, but afterwards it was surprisingly easy to program myself.

3. Then you have to repeat and reinforce the new habit. Reinforcing the habit is important. If you can have a small celebration or reward for getting away from your procrastinating action and moving towards your productive action, then you'll be more likely to get to that productive state in the future.

4. After you've done this for about sixty-six days, you get to unconscious-competence and you're home free. It's easier said than done, but if you can get at least to stage two, then to stage three, you'll be way more productive.

Figure 6: Changing Behaviours and Habits curve[5]

As you can see, it takes effort to become conscious. It takes even more effort to become competent. Habits are a human evolutionary adaptation, as our brain consumes more energy per unit weight compared to any other

---

[5] The Habit loop adapted from Charles Duhigg's *The Power of Habit* overlaid on a grid representation of Abraham Maslow's four stages of competence.

organ. Habits form to conserve the energy our brain uses to make decisions.

If changing your habits or even just getting things done seems like a difficult task, you should try to get rid of your excuses. Or if you can't get rid of excuses, then find a purpose that completely outweighs your excuses. Getting rid of excuses is generally the tougher thing to do. If your habit is snacking, having junk food nearby makes that easy. You can get rid of an excuse to snack by not stocking junk food in the house to help your willpower. Putting off a term paper to watch a show or browse Instagram is typical student behaviour. One way to get rid of excuses and focus on your term paper is to set yourself up in a location without an internet connection, thereby reducing distractions from your task (although your paper probably requires research that you'd be hard pressed to do without the internet). You can already see the challenge with this approach because it focuses on your willpower.

If-then conditioning tries to get you to replace your unwanted behaviour with another that is more positive and productive. Something like if I feel like snacking I will call one of my best friends to catch up instead. Or, if that term paper needs doing but Netflix is calling me, I will curl up with my books (and perhaps a snack to entice me to get going). Again, challenging, but doable.

Generally, however, the most effective way to get past procrastination is to focus on your purpose. If your purpose is greater than your excuses, then those excuses become much easier to overcome. If I were a swimmer training for the Olympics, I wouldn't focus on waking up at 4 a.m. and swimming fifty laps; I would focus on the training helping me get one step closer to my gold medal. Similarly, when working on a term paper, don't focus on the amount of work you need to do; focus on how much more prepared learning this information will make you for the job of your dreams.

You are a collection of your habits, and having good habits will help you find your passion. Exercising, eating right, sleeping, saving, making time for family and friends, or thinking positively can help form a foundation for your future success. Spending time in school is good for practising discipline, and it is a good test of your ability to manage your time and priorities.

Being positive and building good habits doesn't mean you won't think negative thoughts. However, you shouldn't spend more time than you must dealing with those thoughts. Everyone has negative thoughts.

Acknowledge them, then move away from them. Jim Rohn has an interesting technique for dealing with negativity: when you're frustrated, turn it into fascination. This works for me when I remember to use it. For example, if you're frustrated because you're stuck in bumper-to-bumper traffic, think of how amazing it is to have all these cars on the road at the same time. Be fascinated by where everyone might be going, by the effort it took to build so many cars, by the fact that you can push your foot down on a pedal and cause controlled explosions in the engine that move you forward, or by the amount of time and effort it must have taken to put down hundreds or thousands of kilometres of asphalt and concrete for the roads. All of that can be quite fascinating to think about, and focusing on that instead will cause your frustration to fade away.

TRY THIS: Build good habits

Complete assignments in advance. Don't cram. Finish your school commitments before you have fun. Make time to have fun as a reward. Meet obligations. Reflect and learn. Build Meaningful Connections. Be mindful of when you're procrastinating. Look for ways to change your procrastinating behaviours. Leverage if-then conditioning. Focus on your purpose. Turn frustration into fascination. Track your goals and plan to meet them at least 80 percent of the time. Spend an hour reflecting on times of procrastination over the week, and use if-then conditioning for future planning. Be better at noticing those times you start to procrastinate in the moment. Eliminate excuses and focus on purpose to build good habits.

Time management is attention management

Some of the best habits to develop are time management and prioritization. You don't manage time, but you do prioritize (consciously or unconsciously) what you do at any given period. And time is the most precious commodity of all. You could always make more money or buy fancier clothes, a nicer car, a bigger house, but once that second ticks away, it's gone. You can't bank time. So, cherish it. To make the most of your time, start by knowing how you spend it. Then decide if you've made effective use of your time. Most importantly, you must understand where you spend your attention. Time management and prioritization is about *attention management*.

What has your attention? Where are you spending your energy? What are you focusing on? Let's start with prioritization.

Stephen Covey, who wrote the popular self-help book *The 7 Habits of Highly Effective People*, popularized a matrix method of prioritization based on importance and urgency that former US President Dwight D. Eisenhower apparently originated (Covey named the matrix after him, the "Eisenhower Decision Matrix"). The matrix is a four-box figure with "Important" and "Unimportant" along the side, and "Urgent" and "Not Urgent" along the top. See the diagram I've included below. I've added "Significance" to this version of the matrix, calling it the Eisenhower matrix+. The idea of Significance came from Rory Vaden's book, *Procrastinate on Purpose*. Significance is how long something lasts; it increases its importance. Something that happens only once has less Significance than something that happens daily. Evaluating tasks based on a combination of Urgency, Importance, and Significance can help determine where we should spend our time.

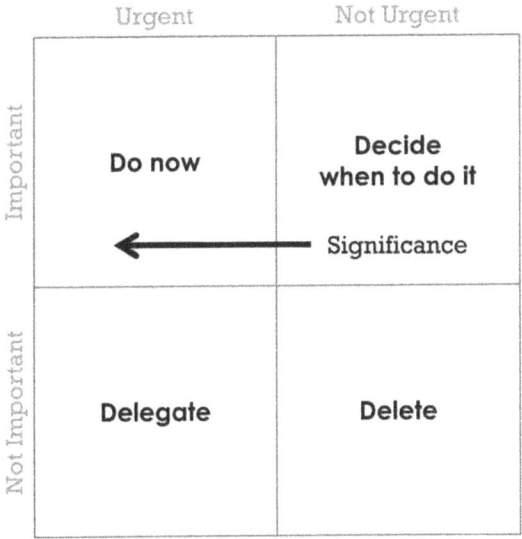

Figure 7: Eisenhower matrix+[6]

---

[6] Adaptation of the Eisenhower Decision Matrix from Stephen Covey represented in grid form with the addition of Rory Vaden's concept of Significance.

For activities that are

- Important and urgent — do them now
    - These activities are straightforward. The smoke alarm in the kitchen is going off. Your baby is crying. Production is down. Do it right away.
- Important and not urgent — decide when to do them
    - These are often the most challenging. You know that you should do them. Unfortunately, you often don't. Here is where you should be spending most of your time (hopefully there aren't too many important and urgent cases to take you away from the important and not urgent ones).
- Not important and urgent — delegate them
    - These are often what "busy" people do occasionally to avoid doing important and not urgent things. Hand these off to others if you're able.
- Not important and not urgent — get rid of them
    - These are often what chronic procrastinators do. They are often entertaining and provide an escape. Spending too much time here is when people are unable to reach their potential as they don't get around to doing what is important. Just don't do these things; if they must get done, then it has some level of importance and should be placed in a different quadrant.
- Significance — add frequency and time to the mix
    - If you only do something once, it has lower Significance. If you do something frequently or for a long time, then it has higher Significance. Thus, something that is not as important but you have to do daily for the next year could be raised to the level of importance because of its frequency.
    - I also include effect on energy level as part of Significance. There are activities you do that increase

your energy level, and you should consider increasing their value on the Significance scale since that added energy will help you do more.

Think of it like a points system. Urgent tasks get more points than tasks that aren't urgent. Important tasks get more points than tasks that aren't important. Significance can be a multiplier of Urgency and Importance points. You'll have to come up with how many points something is and what each Significance multiplier is based on your circumstances.

So now that we have a rough idea of how to prioritize, we should look at how much time to spend on each task. I'm offering a few rough general rules that should be adjusted on a case-by-case basis. These rules can still help you see if you are spending enough time on your academics.

Here's an illustrative example: A typical university course load is five courses. You should aim to spend about eight hours per week per course. The typical work week is about forty hours. Now isn't that convenient? The difference is that you might have early classes or late classes, with some classes clustered together then long breaks between others. From Monday to Friday there are 120 hours. We're assuming that you take weekends off. Take out eight hours per day for sleep and that leaves you with eighty hours. Take out forty hours for school and that still leaves you forty hours. During those remaining forty hours, you need to eat and exercise. This is also time you can spend reading, consuming content to improve yourself, learning a new skill, volunteering, working a part-time job, starting your own project on the side, and then, once in a while, taking some time to decompress with TV, YouTube, gaming, or something else less productive.

What about time with friends and family? Use the forty-eight hours during the weekend for that. What if you want to spend time with them during the week? If you want to do that, why not borrow some of those hours from the weekend? Go out on a Thursday night and spend the equivalent hours Saturday afternoon investing in yourself.

Time is your most precious resource. Well, unless you have a time machine (and if you do, call me, I want in). You can't manage time (i.e., you can't make more of it). What you can do is manage your priorities and how you're spending your attention.

So, when managing your attention, energy, and focus, you'll want to start by:

1. Knowing where you spend your time.
2. Prioritizing what you spend your time on.
3. Focusing your energy on those priorities (giving your full attention where possible).

Eat the biggest frog first

Brian Tracy, a self-development author, combines the concepts of prioritization, getting things done, and willpower when he says, "eat your frog first." The concept likely comes from Mark Twain, who is credited with saying, "Eat a live frog first thing in the morning and nothing worse will happen to you the rest of the day." So, if you have picked and prioritized your goal for the day, and it's staring at you like a frog that you know you must eat, then doing it at the end of the day will be taxing on your willpower. So, when Brian tells you to "eat your frog first," and you find you have a lot of frogs to eat, Mark Twain has a quote to help you out: "If it's your job to eat a frog, it's best to do it first thing in the morning. And if it's your job to eat two frogs, it's best to eat the biggest one first."

Like many others, I love my sleep. I would make a game of how late I could wake up to get to work at a certain time. That made the day more stressful and made it more likely that my willpower would be spent before I could complete important tasks. So, when I got home, and I still had to get something done then it probably seemed a lot like Mark Twain's large, live frog staring me down, waiting to be eaten. It was often difficult to muster up the courage to do so, and instead I'd leave the frog where it was to sit there taunting me.

Taking matters into my own hands and trying something different, I decided to get to sleep an hour earlier and wake up an hour earlier. In this way, I reduced my excuses and could chow down on the frog first thing in the morning with minimal hesitation.

Pick your Big Rocks

I often hear people say, "There aren't enough hours in the day." And while that may be true, you should also understand that everyone is given the same twenty-four hours, and that people choose to spend that time in very different ways. You can't manage time since you can't create more, and prioritization just takes your to-do list and rearranges it. So, getting the most out of your time is really about managing your energy and focus.

It's often good to understand where you spend your energy, so doing a time audit is helpful for some people. Then you can compare how much of your day is spent on productive versus non-productive things. Then you should consider where you want to spend your time.

I often share the Stephen Covey story of the "Big Rocks." To paraphrase:

> *A professor goes in front of his class with a large glass jar and starts putting fist-sized rocks inside. He asks the class, "Is the jar full? Raise your hand if you think so." The class is unsure, but a few hands go up. He goes under his desk and takes out some gravel, and starts pouring gravel into the jar. It falls between the large rocks, taking up the remaining space in the jar. He again asks the class who thinks the jar is full. A few more hands go up. He takes out some sand and pours it in the jar. It starts filling in the spaces between the rocks. The professor asks again, "Who thinks the jar is full?" A few more hands go up. Then he pours water into the jar and again asks, "Is the jar full?" Well yes, the jar is full.*
>
> *He asks the class, "What's the point of this illustration?" Someone puts up their hand and says, "No matter how many hours there are in the day, you can always cram more in there," and the class starts nodding in agreement. The professor speaks up and says, "No, absolutely not! The point is that if you didn't start with the big rocks, you wouldn't have fit everything in."*

Too many people are focused on gravel (that meeting you didn't need to attend, that person you could have cut off at fifteen minutes instead of spending thirty to catch up), sand (the YouTube video that was mildly informational, or that *Game of Thrones* episode), and water (those 9gag.com images or Reddit threads you didn't have to spend time looking at).

Now imagine that each day you do one important thing. Just one. Doing just one important thing a day will mean that you get 365 important things done each year. And the beauty of it is that I'm sure you can do more than one important thing a day. So, focusing on Big Rocks can help you be much more effective and keep you on your road to reaching your career potential.

Eisenhower matrix+

Use the Eisenhower matrix+ as a prioritization tool. Print out a copy and hang it in your work area. Save it to your phone's camera roll. Make sure it's easily accessible. When you have to make a decision to do something, put it in the matrix to see how you should handle it.

Ivey Lee productivity method

American publicity expert and consultant Ivy Lee came up with a productivity technique in the early 1900s for Charles Schwab, a successful businessman at the time. Lee said to write down the six most important things to do today, to focus on the first task until it's done, then focus on the next, and so on. If any tasks are unfinished at the end of the day, move them to tomorrow's list. Then repeat daily. For that simple approach, Schwab reportedly gave Lee $25,000 (which would be about $400,000 today) for the fifteen minutes that Lee spent with Schwab's executives to help increase the efficiency of the team. Not a bad haul for only a quarter of an hour's worth of work.

Whatever system you use, understand that your Big Rocks can be rearranged and continued focus will lead to more productivity.

Make your goals SMART

Defining your goals with the SMART characteristics can help you achieve them. SMART is an acronym for:

- Specific: As Jim Rohn said, "Ambiguous goals produce ambiguous results." Don't give yourself room to wiggle out.

- Measurable: Peter Drucker said, "What gets measured, gets managed." Similarly, your goals can't be considered achieved unless you can measure them (even by proxy). Spell out what you consider a success before you get there.

- Attainable: Your goals should challenge you, but they should still be achievable. They should be just far enough away that striving towards them gets you out of your comfort zone and makes you grow.

- Realistic: Combine the other attributes so that you can reasonably achieve the goal. Dropping ten pounds is specific, measurable, and attainable, and doing that over ten weeks should be doable, but if you wanted to do it in ten days, that might not be realistic.

- Time Bound: Giving yourself a due date makes sure that you don't drag out achieving your goals forever.

Use WOOP to set your goals

If you are not able to achieve your goals, then perhaps you need to WOOP it. The WOOP construct was created by Gabriele Oettingen, Professor of Psychology at New York University and the University of Hamburg. WOOP stands for Wish, Outcome, Obstacle, Plan. WOOP goals are like SMART goals, but with a slightly different purpose. WOOP focuses on the purpose and obstacles to help you "program" yourself with a plan to achieve your wish.

- Wish: What do you want to do?

- Outcome: What is your best outcome? What do you want to achieve? These are your results, which often answer your "Why?"

- Obstacle: What is your *inner* obstacle that prevents you from fulfilling your wish? Do you have a bad habit, belief, or emotion that is getting in the way?

- Plan: What can you do to overcome the obstacle? Often you can make a plan using if-then statements — "If <obstacle>, then <what you're going to do about it.>

From the information on purpose and habits, you can understand why WOOP would work for many, as you're taking the outcome and assigning a purpose to it to understand your motivation. Obstacles are then overcome by reprogramming the associated habits into new ones.

TRY THIS: Experiment with time management and prioritization

Test your time management and prioritization. Print out a copy of the Eisenhower matrix+ (Figure 7 in Chapter 8). Divide the plan part of your WOOP into smaller goals. Make those goals SMART goals. Use any or all *TRY THIS* challenges as ten-day challenges. Make the goals more ambitious, and stretch them to twenty days. Increase up to sixty-six days. This way, they are sure to become habits. Define your goals using the WOOP and SMART acronyms.

Habits learned early will contribute to your success. One of the best predictors of success isn't IQ, it's the ability to delay gratification. Young people who score high on tests that verify their ability to delay gratification are more likely to be successful in life. This makes sense because if you're not focused on short-term gains, then you can make longer-term investments that will pay off later.

TRY THIS: Schedule your social media time

Social media seems to be a strong time thief and if you're finding that getting lost in social media is a challenge for you, one interesting productivity hack is to schedule time for it. Acknowledge that you need the time, and give yourself the time, but if you're on your social sites outside of your scheduled times, stop and disconnect. Tell yourself that you'll have time to procrastinate later.

Chapter 9: Job Hunt

I was in my last year of university, and pressure to find a job was high. I had my resume prepared for my previous co-op terms, so it just needed to be updated with my most recent work experience and the little that I had done during my previous academic term. Then came the application process.

Properly navigating the job-hunt process would be SIWIKE that I would provide myself. Here is what I have learned through recruiting for several years. Processes for different companies will have their variations, but most are similar to Figure 8.

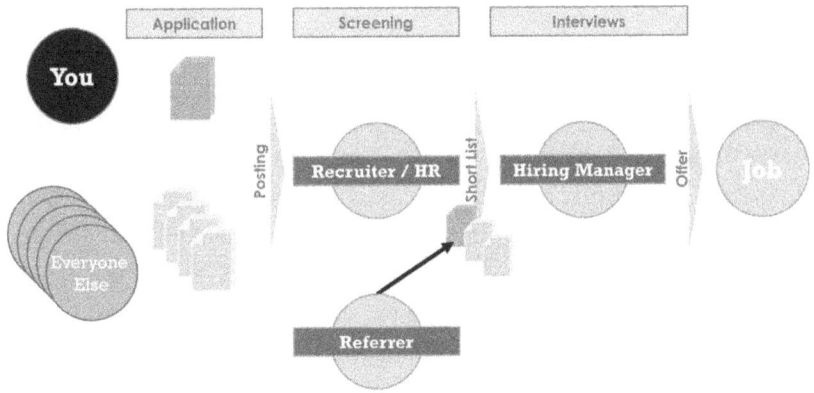

Figure 8: Hiring process

This is an oversimplification of the hiring process, but it is a good illustration of how hiring typically happens. You apply online — along with tens, hundreds, perhaps thousands of others. The posting goes into a system — email for smaller companies or an applicant tracking system for larger ones. A recruiter screens the submitted resumes to produce a short list. Someone within the company might refer a candidate during this process, and this person will likely end up on the short list. The hiring manager and their team interview the candidate. And if any candidates are successful, they get an offer of employment.

It's important to recognize that there is a difference between a recruiter and a hiring manager. In a smaller company, one person might take on both roles, but in most medium- to large-size companies, the recruiter and the hiring manager often work in two different groups. So, if you're the networking type, you want to get through to the hiring manager, if possible, although the recruiter is often the gatekeeper. You could also make your way in through a referral.

It is worth noting that recruiters come in different forms:

- External recruiters who work on commission (often called headhunters) scout the market to fill roles in different companies.

- External recruiters who are kept on retainer (meaning they get a flat rate per recruitment period), work almost like an extension of the company.

- Internal recruiters work for the company.

Recruiters often have limited information on the role they are recruiting for. If they haven't previously recruited for that role, the recruiter needs to match the role and the applicant based on whatever the hiring manager gives them, and for inexperienced recruiters, the specific words on applications matter a lot. A hiring manager might understand that some of the terms you use on your application are equivalent, but a new recruiter might not know this and end up passing on you for another candidate. So, if you have experience "addressing clients' concerns," which to you is the same as "customer service," you leave it up to the recruiter's quick one-minute scan of your resume to consider them the same. To help the recruiter check all the necessary boxes and pass your application on to the hiring manager, tweak your wording so it matches the job advertisement.

A recruiter often goes through hundreds if not thousands of resumes for each process. Resumes all start to look basically the same. I'm sure you've heard the myth that a recruiter spends an average of thirty seconds reviewing a resume. The process a recruiter typically follows is putting resumes into "No", "Yes", and "Maybe" piles and then looking at some resumes in more detail. The recruiter will have a good sense of what a "No" resume looks like, and they often won't take six seconds to look at one, let alone thirty. In fact, resume screening tends to be more on how to disqualify someone from getting interviewed than on how to qualify them. Spelling and grammar errors, misaligned text or bullets, mismatched font and spacing, might not seem like a big deal to you, but to someone who is reviewing a few hundred resumes, these things stand out and give them an excuse to junk your resume. From their perspective, if you aren't willing to put effort into such a seemingly simple thing on something that is supposed to represent your best work, you likely won't be willing to put the appropriate effort into the job. So, put your best effort in to avoid being placed in the "No" pile.

A "Yes" resume could take some time to review. Sometimes resumes are an obvious "Yes," so the decision can be quick. For others, it's not so clear. A single role, depending on its seniority, will likely warrant three to five final candidates in the process. So more than five resumes in the "Yes" pile means the recruiter must rule out some. There may also be too few in the "Yes" pile, meaning that the recruiter might want to go into the "Maybe" pile to find the top few candidates to be interviewed.

When the recruiter tries to eliminate resumes from the "Yes" or "Maybe" piles, they often compare two at a time to see which is better, and then take out unwanted candidates. It's sometimes not the bottom candidate that gets eliminated in this way, since if several candidates have the same skill set and one gets rejected by the hiring manager, they will likely all get rejected. But if a few have different profiles (e.g., one has more technical skills and one has more leadership experience), then there is a higher likelihood that all won't be rejected.

Everyone is a salesperson

Sales is a skill that everyone needs. Maybe not to sell a product or service, but perhaps to convince someone to eat at a certain restaurant or watch a certain movie. We all need to influence others sometimes, and being a better influencer can be an acquired skill that might be very helpful in progressing in the world. Being able to influence others to select one of your ideas, or use one of the approaches you suggested, or hire someone you suggest are all a form of sales. Pretty much getting anyone to do anything you suggest to them is sales, which makes sales a very useful skill to have.

Don't like selling? A mentor told me that "selling is just problem solving," which made sense to me. Instead of selling someone something, look to solve their problem. You'll have a good shot at selling your goods or services if you make their problem go away. I am not a salesperson myself, but I am learning every day. For example, I like helping others, so having someone sign up for a coaching package is not selling them something, it's providing a solution to catalyze and accelerate their success. Don't sell, just add value.

TRY THIS: Reframe selling

Reflect on times you had to convince someone of something this past week. Frame the "sale" within a perspective that suits your abilities.

In every role, there is a "customer" to be served

Service typically speaks to the value that you bring to the customer. In an entrepreneurial environment, customers that don't see value don't stay customers for long. Your goal is to continue to deliver value whether you interact with the customer or not.

Any job you do has a "customer." That customer might not be a person paying for a product or service. It could be someone in another department in the company or even your boss.

TRY THIS: Find the customer in whatever you do

Reflect on times where you had to do an especially challenging or rewarding task this past week. Who was your customer? What could you have done better? How could you have made the experience even more rewarding for your customer?

Reverse-engineer the job you want

When I was looking for a job, I wanted to work as either a network administrator or a developer. I put those key words into the job sites and got technology companies like IBM, Microsoft, Sun, or others. The job I finally landed after university was at Deloitte (one of the Big Four accounting firms, though I worked in the technology practice under the management consulting service), and my title was Associate. I do not recall the role ever coming up in my job search results. I did not think too much of it at the time. As I was reflecting on reverse-engineering all the "lucky" accidents that happened in my career, I realized that the job never appeared because I was searching for job titles instead of the role. In a technical job, the title often reflects the role. The title is what your position is called, and often it does not reflect what you actually do. Your role is what you do on a regular basis.

I encourage my mentees to understand the role they want. Many business students will mistake their specializations with the roles they want as a job. Business students want finance, management, or economics jobs, for example. Understanding the role first is important because the title might be a little misleading. You should focus on the responsibilities of the job, especially as there is not necessarily consistency in titles across companies.

TRY THIS: Find a role to focus on

Spend time thinking of roles you would shortlist as potential future jobs. Validate your understanding of the role by connecting with someone actually doing it.

Focus on accomplishments, not activities, on your resume

Many people dread working on their resume. Because it isn't a true reflection of the person applying, it is not a very effective tool. But it is a reality of today that must be addressed. You might be interested to know that the resume is a relatively recent invention that only became commonplace around the 1950s. So it's only about as old as your grandparents (and it honestly hasn't evolved much since then). Before then, you were hired because you knew someone — a local farmer, the innkeeper, or the blacksmith. And if you go further back, before the modern education system, the only way you could learn was to be an apprentice. The understanding was that you knew nothing and you were taught the job. As society became more connected because of larger cities and faster transportation, more people were around and available to work, which changed how people were hired. If a company wanted to hire the right person, they started to look at multiple candidates to find the best fit for the job. Cover letters were added to provide some context around the applicant. Together, the resume and cover letter allowed the hiring process to be streamlined by allowing hiring managers to deal with a higher volume of people by reviewing the summaries of their work experience.

So what's important about a resume today? Let me demystify the process by going through the recruitment process. The recruiter is the first person to see your application at a given company. Recruiters receive hundreds if not thousands of applications, and the candidates may or may not be qualified, but they all found the posting and applied. Some application tracking systems do some basic filtering, but most companies don't rely on complex algorithms; people are still doing the screening (although that may change as natural language processing technologies improve). Recruiters will evaluate a typical entry-level candidate based on their school and program of study. Some will ask for transcripts to see your GPA.

Unfortunately, there is no universal, "correct" way to write a resume. However, I have developed the FOCUS Inspired Resume Model as a baseline. If you're going to use a resume, at least follow these guidelines, which probably 90 percent of recruiters will agree with.

The cover letter is sometimes an optional part of the application that is often not well understood. I am often asked by candidates whether they should submit a cover letter if it is not required. My answer is always yes. You should take any opportunity to tell them more about yourself since that's what you're selling. The cover letter should not summarize your resume; it's your opportunity to tell the recruiter or hiring manager about you, explain why you are interested in the company, and describe what value you will bring to the company. If any points on your resume need explanation, the cover letter could do that. But less is more — keep it short, clear, and concise. Now let's see how these documents factor into the process.

TRY THIS: Update your resume

Set a calendar appointment to update your resume every three to four months.

Practice your interview skills

Interviews exist because of job volume and accessibility. The days of hiring only the people you knew well and training them as apprentices are long past. There are so many more ways of finding people, and schools and other institutions have replaced apprenticeships as a way for job seekers to get knowledge and experience. We know about the resume's role. The interview is the last bit of human evaluation to come before you are given a job.

Details: Guidelines for a great interview

Interviews come in a few forms:

- Behavioural — focus on your past performance.

- Technical or functional — focus on the specific skills required for the job.
- Case — assess how you'd manage a situation that approximates something you'd encounter in the job.

When you get a job interview, you'll want to make sure you prepare as much as you can and have the following things ready:

1. Know yourself: Be able to talk through any and all of the experience on your resume. If you've followed the FIRM approach to your resume (as discussed below in the "FOCUS Inspired Resume Model" section), you'll be well on your way, since you not only know the activities that you did, but how those achievements demonstrated value to the company you worked for. Sometimes during interviews, when I've asked candidates to elaborate on a bullet point on their resume, they will say they forgot it was there. Something that is supposed to represent the best and most appropriate demonstration of how good a candidate you would be for the job, and you forgot? It seems quite unprofessional.

2. Know the company: Being able to answer the typical "why us" question in a manner that is more than just having read the "about" section of the website is important. Taking the time to understand what value the company could provide to you and more importantly what value you could provide to the company. Knowing the company means knowing the marketplace, including their competitors. Has the company been in the news recently? Is the industry the company is in doing well or not? Do you or someone you know use the products or services of the company? Of a competitor? What challenges or opportunities might the company have in the future? What about the company makes you want to work for them? Think about it as interviewing the company. Why should you work for them? Knowing answers to these questions shows that you are interested and informed about the company, and that you have the potential to add more value. Making an effort to know the company will go a long way, and the interviewers will see this.

3. Practice: This seems like an easy one, but it's not necessarily done well. Interviewers expect you to come prepared. Being able to answer the "top twenty" interview questions from your favourite search engine is not enough. Practicing on your own is the minimum you should do, and if that's all you can do, then at least record yourself (use your phone to record the answer to your questions). Do you have any physical or verbal tics? Work on correcting them as they might distract the interviewer. Another useful piece of advice is to not watch the video until the day after you record. By doing so you remove the context that was in your head as you were answering the questions to make sure that the answer makes sense on its own. Ideally, ask a friend or a career advisor to watch you or the video and provide their feedback and perspective. Do you want a preview of the questions the interviewer will likely ask? Take a look at the job posting. Points listed in the job posting will likely make it into the interview questions, so those should be your areas of focus. Also be prepared to answer questions about the experiences listed on your resume.

4. Logistics: Make sure that you are well-versed on the location of the interview and any other details that you need to take care of well in advance (including planning out your attire and dressing appropriately). Plan to arrive thirty minutes early, but then only actually arrive ten to fifteen minutes early; you don't want to put any unnecessary pressure on your interviewer).

Above and beyond knowing the company, doing your "homework" is about getting to know other people in the company, perhaps even learning about your interviewer or the group that you're being hired into, the culture of the company, or any other useful information about the company or your role.

I'm often contacted by someone who is frantically excited that they have an interview, but because they haven't practiced periodically for interviews beforehand, I end up having to provide a crash course on interviewing. It can be challenging for them to remember everything for later that week, sometimes even the next day. Being proactive about the interview prep process is important, especially for students who are in the thick of hiring season. They should be practicing and preparing all through the application process whether they have an interview or not. That way, even if they don't get an interview, the prep will help them for future jobs (or at the very least be practice for public or semi-private speaking).

If you have already graduated and are applying for jobs, you should be practicing well ahead of being given an interview. Additionally, you may want to schedule a periodic practice every three to six months, regardless of whether you have a job or not, for the potential ad-hoc headhunting that will inevitably come your way throughout your career.

TRY THIS: Practice interviewing

Periodically practice your interview skills. Every semester (perhaps as you update your career document), spend twenty minutes refreshing your interview responses.

Hiring is seasonal — know when to apply

Many reach out to me with an interest in applying for roles in consulting (based on my background) only to find out that postings were now closed. It is important to know when companies are hiring. Many professional services companies (consulting, accounting, and banking) look for candidates a whole year in advance. That means you should be preparing and applying in September of your graduating year for a job that might not start until the next September. Other companies are a few months ahead (e.g., summer internships sometimes take applications in January, while others require you to apply in September or October of the previous year). In any case, do some due diligence to understand the hiring cycle long before you need the job so that you can be well-prepared.

TRY THIS: Build a list of peak seasons

Reach out to recruiters, senior students, or alumni who know something about the jobs you want and ask about recruiting seasons for the role. Make a calendar of peak hiring seasons over the next year or so.

Work experience is the shortcut to going pro

Do you know how to swim? If you don't, then pretend you do. When learning how to swim, did you read the book on swimming? Of course not. You were probably in the pool floating, holding your breath, moving your arms, kicking your feet, and otherwise practicing. So why should experience in your future job be restricted to your academic school experience?

Go out there and get work experience. If you have the option of work-integrated learning, then that's great. If not, then go get an internship over the summer. Or get volunteer experience. Or start something on your own to become a practitioner.

TRY THIS: Get experience

Get work experience. Paid or unpaid. If you're not in a formal co-op or internship program, leverage your summers (if you can't work for all of it, work for at least three of the four months). Sprinkle in some volunteer work part-time. Build Meaningful Connections (BMC) with multiple people in your field of specialization every week. Work at least one summer while you're in post-secondary school (and ideally also in secondary school) in your field of specialization.

When you go through your internship, "pre-write" your resume. Plan what you want to accomplish in the next six to twelve months. Assuming you have a job and are at least meeting expectations, ask your manager for more experience. Some managers might allow you to work with another group if your regular responsibilities have been taken care of.

Your job hunt never ends

Being open to opportunities could have changed my life. Unfortunately, I was like most people. I was either "on" the job hunt or "off." Instead I should have been open to opportunities. That means periodically taking a quick look at the jobs in the marketplace and regularly connecting with your network. Then you should examine what others are doing that might be interesting for you. That interest could turn into a future opportunity. Being open to opportunities was not something I did, but I could have changed myself. You should be open to opportunities and have your life changed.

When you're open to opportunities, you are working to demonstrate results, as well as planning for future results to get you to the next stage of your career. You are pre-writing your resume every three to four months and making the effort to keep your resume up to date at the same time. That way you can make minor modifications every few months instead of writing whole sections trying to remember what you did years ago. Plus, scan the job market just to see what jobs out there might be of interest to you. And if any jobs are of interest, make the effort to apply to them.

On the relationship side, you are periodically connecting with your network and continuously building your network. Your curiosity is out in full force and you are continuously looking for ways to add value. That value has the potential to be returned many times over after you build your meaningful connections and occasionally ask your network to help you out.

So, don't be complacent. Make the effort to be open to opportunities.

TRY THIS: Track your job hunt

Most people network to find a job. While that may be an important reason to network, the true value of networking will reveal itself far out in the future. After you and your classmates graduate from the same program, you go to your job and they go to theirs. Where are they in five years? Ten years? Twenty years? Some will be successful, some won't. And those won't necessarily correspond to the people that you thought would be successful either.

Many people I speak to will say something like "I wish I stayed in touch with..." referring to someone at school or a previous job. So, take that SIWIKE and try to stay connected with everyone. If the person doesn't reciprocate, don't force it, but a quick email, text, or phone call will go a long way.

Gain experience managing up, beside, and below

As you move further up, you will typically have more decisions to make, potentially in less time. Realize too that your boss also likely has many demands on their time. Being able to manage up, beside and below are skills that are extremely useful to showcase on your resume.

To effectively manage around you, you need clear and concise communication. Understanding where you and your boss are in relation to the DISC model is useful. You will want to try to keep your boss's needs in mind. In a communication to an executive, information should be prioritized. The US marines have implemented a technique called BLUF (Bottom Line Up Front) where you take the typical concluding sentence (which would contain your requested decision or call to action) and move that to the front. Any additional information can be provided at the end, after the reader understands what you are the requesting.

Consider this scenario:

A bus driver named Dave picks up three passengers at the first bus station. One is in a wheelchair.

He goes to the next stop and picks up five passengers (one that needs walking assistance with a cane) and two get off. He goes to the next stop where three passengers get on and four get off (including the person in the wheelchair, causing a slight delay as they wait for the bus ramp to deploy). At the next stop, no one gets off and three people get on (including another person with a cane). The next stop, a family with a stroller and one toddler gets on, and one person gets off. The next stop one person with a bicycle gets on and two people get off. At the last station, four people get off, including the person with the bicycle.

What was the name of the bus driver?

The expected question would be, "How many people are left on the bus?" Knowing the question by having the BLUF would have made the response easy. However, not knowing communication's purpose or the decision to be made makes answering the question more challenging than it needs to be. As an employee, you might have communications with your boss where you're not sure what they're asking of you or where you are confused about what they're trying to say. If you try to put yourself in their shoes and think about what they might want in their current situation, you attempt to "guess the context" and gain a better understanding of what they want. Often, though, it is best to ask for clarification. Knowing what is expected of you is important, and sometimes all it takes is asking.

For example, your mom asks you to clean up the living room. You look at the living room and you make the assumption that she wanted a clean house. So, you spend a long time dusting and vacuuming, and a bit of time putting things into the boxes around the room. You make sure there is no dirt or dust around. She comes back and is upset with you, asking you why you didn't clean up the living room. Confused, you ask what she meant by "clean the living room," and you discover that what she wanted was for the room to look more spacious. She didn't even expect you to vacuum or dust, which is where you spent most of your time. All she really wanted you to do was to take those boxes and move them into the basement.

Additionally, from DISC you know that some people are more "task focused" whereas some are "people focused." Many absolutely prefer a quick two-minute conversation versus a multi-page email. So, understanding that preference is also key to effective communication. In today's world, live communication can happen via phone, video conference, or instant messenger. In person might be best, but it is not always possible, so you want to be able to use whatever interactive communication method they prefer.

When referring to the frequency of communication, only a few bosses would hold "too much communication" against you (if you're not deliberately being a pest), especially when you are new at a job. Most would hold "not enough communication" against you though, particularly if a few questions might have saved you from making a mistake or wasting time.

But it's not just about communication between you and your boss. Often you have to work as a part of a larger team. When I talk about managing "beside," I mean that decisions are frequently made by groups of peers. Consensus decisions that seem to happen easily often start way earlier. The decision often takes the path of doing a "roadshow" to all the relevant people to get buy in and incorporate any concerns well ahead of the final decision. Before going a few levels up, even though your boss is onboard, you often need to make sure that your boss's peers are onboard as well. You want to make sure that you have the support of those impacted by the recommendation or decision, so you can focus on the decision versus the details. This means that the road to decision usually isn't just the thirty minutes in the decision meeting; it's the three weeks ahead of the meeting where you reached out to your boss and her three peers (meaning you needed to connect with your six peers first) to get feedback, then circled back before the recommendation was presented and the final decision made.

When managing your peers, many of the same principles apply as managing up. BLUF communications are useful. Understanding their verbal and reading communication preferences is important. Do they prefer over-communication rather than under-communication? And then adapt your "roadshow" as appropriate.

There will always be some co-workers who are more vocal than others, so-called "squeaky wheels." And there will be ones who are more influential regardless of how vocal they are. So, pay special attention to peers you put in those categories.

At some point, you'll move up. You may need to manage people who are reporting to you. You now get to be at the receiving end of the previous management points. Remember how you felt to be the one reporting. What would you want your boss to do for you to enable you to be effective in your work? You might have to look to your EQ to see beyond what your own needs were and focus on what they would want you to do for them. Now the answer is slightly different depending on how you are but will always have the following elements.

- Set expectations: Start by setting clear expectations of the person you are supervising. If they are creating the deliverable, what are the parameters of the report? When is it due? What should it contain? Whose input is needed? If they are in an operational role, what are their targets? How many, how fast, at what rating? When setting expectations, first help your direct report understand what your expectations are. If your idea of a good rate is twelve per hour and your report thinks it is ten per hour, then there is misalignment. If you need it by Friday, but your report thinks you need it tomorrow, expectations are misaligned again.

- Understand constraints: Some constraints are set by the expectations imposed. However, there may be other constraints. If your report only works on your deliverable, it might be quite reasonable for them to get it to you on Friday. However, if they have other work in progress, something assigned by someone else, you will want to understand what those other constraints are and potentially realign expectations appropriately. Personal constraints may also need to be considered. Your report might have family commitments that may challenge the expectations. Being aware of and understanding those constraints is important, not necessarily because you need to concede to them, but so you can work towards a mutually appropriate arrangement.

- Provide mentorship guidance: Depending on the time frame of the project, setting a check-in date to provide some mentorship and guidance may be appropriate. You might not need to be the one checking in. You could nominate someone for your report to turn to if assistance is needed. Also, establishing an environment where questions are encouraged is beneficial.

Looking at your reports and considering the support you'd want from your boss should also help you round out how you manage your boss and peers.

TRY THIS: Practice managing

Find opportunities at school, in your volunteer roles, and at your work to manage those above you, your peers, or anyone you might need to manage.

Essential tips and tools for job seekers

The job shopping list

The first thing you'll want to do is develop your shopping list for your job search. The "job shopping list" is basically the must-haves and the nice-to-haves of the jobs you are searching for. Most start their job search based on their industry, function, and geography. For those and other attributes of your shopping list consider what is important to you.

- Industry: Most students focus on their industry. I am in finance, so I should work at a bank. I am in computers, so should work for a company in Silicon Valley. I'm an accountant, so I should work at one of the Big Four.

- Function: Plenty of companies in other industries need finance people, or people who understand computers or can do accounting. I was initially narrowly focused on coding jobs at tech companies and was fortunate to find a coding role at a management consulting firm.

- Geography: You might be very motivated to stay in the city where you studied or grew up. But if a job in another city, province, state, or country came up, would you consider it? Most people probably would. So, is working locally is a "must-have" or just a "nice-to-have"?

- Related disciplines: Many roles are interdisciplinary, and you might have only studied one part. Let's say your degree is in psychology. You might know that marketing has an extensive psychology element based on consumer attention and behaviour. So, that degree in psychology could potentially be extended into a role in marketing. Engineering has a core problem solving element, so any job that requires the ability to analyze problems and come up with solutions such as consulting could use the knowledge gained through an engineering degree.

Need more inspiration on roles to consider? Find your degree's alumni and see what they are doing or have done. See if you can manage a coffee or lunch with them, and ask a lot of questions about their career journey. (Oh, and make sure you always offer to pay; they may decline, but at least make the offer.) Make it clear you aren't doing it with the expectation of getting a job. Just be authentically curious.

When just graduating school, you probably want to be a little relaxed with most of your shopping list. Most should be nice-to-haves with few must-haves. As you gain more and more experience, you can start reflecting on which nice-to-haves need to become must-haves so your role provides happiness, fulfillment, and meaning to you. Don't start doing that too early as the early stages of your career should very much be a time for exploration, and taking the bad with the good is often an effective way of getting a larger breadth of experience.

Tracking job applications

The job hunt often takes time and keeping track of key information is important. We recommend you do the following:

1. Download the job posting.
    a. Job postings often contain useful information about the position, but companies might take down their postings or make them inaccessible to the public once the application date has passed. If you only have the link, you might be in trouble if you want to review the posting later.
2. Record information about the job:
    a. Job number (if provided on the posting).

b. The original website address.

c. The resume you used (which might be different for each job if you are tailoring it as we suggest in the "FOCUS Inspired Resume Model" section below).

d. The date when it was posted along with recent interactions (when you applied, when you got a call back, etc.).

e. Comments on status along with other notes (such as the recruiter name, any notes you want to take about the company and the role based on research you've done, any people that you've BMCd with — this could be split up into multiple columns, but we leave it as "comments" in the example for simplicity).

You can do this in Excel, leverage any multitude of online tools, or do it the old-fashioned way and re-create this handy template:

Job #	Website	Resume version	Dates	Comments

Figure 9: Sample job tracking sheet

Your career document

The first time you create your career document will take a while. If you don't update it regularly, each update will take up a lot of time. Aim to update it once a semester.

We recommend you update your career document every year, ideally every three to six months, even if you're not on the job hunt. You will thank yourself since it's much harder to remember what you did after three to six years versus what you did in the past three to six months.

FOCUS Inspired Resume Model

There is no global standard for resumes. The FOCUS Inspired Resume Model (FIRM) is meant to help upgrade everyone's resume. You can choose to do whatever you want with your career document. We simply provide you with a list of recommendations and the rationale for each, so you can make your own decision on what is important.

1. One page please: Unless the job posting has pages and pages of qualifications and requirements, you should be able to spell out your qualifications on one page.

    a. As a recruiter, most of the time I'm looking for a reason to say no or a reason to say yes. If I've already reached the end of the first page and haven't found a compelling reason to say yes, it is highly unlikely I will find a compelling reason on the second page.

    b. Many recruiters will accept a two-page resume, so if you have tons of relevant experience and there are lots of requirements in the job listing, make it two pages. But make sure the most important and relevant information is on the first page. Just know that some recruiters are turned off by a resume that is more than two pages and will not even review it as a result.

    c. Outside of North America, a curriculum vitae (also known as a CV) may be requested. A CV can be ten pages and is the detailed chronicle of your career. Newcomers often struggle when they have a CV from their home country, but they are routinely rejected in the North American market. So, if you are an international student or are getting recommendations from those who have worked abroad, make sure you understand the difference in requirements. There are exceptions, such as academia and research, where they will want a CV.

2. Get rid of the "summary of X" and "objectives" sections.
    a. "Resume" in French means "summary," and your resume is a summary of your career experience. You must think the recruiter doesn't know what they are doing if you think they need a summary of a summary. Plus, without the context on where you got the experience, most of what is in the summary is hollow, not to mention redundant. What about an objective statement? Most recruiters and hiring managers I've spoken to agree that what you want matters less than what you can do for the company. And what you can do for the company should be articulated in your cover letter or in your listed experience. What about a highlights section? The only good argument I've heard for a highlights section is that it helps companies without a dedicated human resource staff where the hiring manager is the recruiter. But if you do have a highlights section, make sure the context is apparent and avoid duplication.
    b. So, include the information as part of the experience when it was obtained.
    c. Also, getting rid of it frees up a lot of space to get you to one page.
3. Activities and Achievements: You need to differentiate yourself. Focus on achievements.
    a. Most resumes outline activities (responsibilities) and "what you did" at your last job. Unfortunately, that says nothing about how well you did it. What separates you from the other candidates are the achievements (accomplishments) and "how well you did it."
    b. This is usually the hardest part of the resume feedback to implement as most people don't do their jobs thinking in terms of achievements. They often don't ask themselves "how do I know if I am doing a good job?" Taking that perspective helps people become better employees.

c. For instance
   i. If your job is to make widgets, a typical resume would have a bullet point that says "made widgets." Okay, great. You as the employee of the month made widgets. The person who was fired for underperforming also made widgets. If you put your recruiter hat on and think about it, without further context you could interpret it in both ways.
   ii. So you update with a number to show how well you did, and you say "made 100 widgets per hour." You're getting closer, but how do I know if 100 widgets per hour is good? If the average is eighty widgets, then you're great. Twenty-five percent above the benchmark. If the average is 125 widgets per hour, then not so much. Again, without knowing whether 100 or ten is good or not, you might get the wrong impression, especially if the recruiter is used to those working in a more automated facility where 1,000 might be the benchmark.
   iii. So, what about "recognized as top performer by exceeding widget production by 25 percent"? It's harder for a recruiter to interpret that negatively. They also might conclude that if you could do 25 percent more at your previous placement, you might be able to turn 1,000 units to 1,250 units per hour at their more automated facility.
   iv. Typically, an achievement follows the structure <Verb><what you accomplished / what were your results><how did you do it>. The "how did you do it" is optional, and the order of the last two could be reversed. If you do reverse things, however, make this consistent across the whole resume.
   v. The convention is to have achievements as bullets and separated from activities. Set activities as sentence fragments without bullets. Set achievements as bullets.

4. Answer the question: So, what?
    a. Yes, it was nice that you won the spelling bee, and yes, running ten kilometres in under an hour is an accomplishment, but if it doesn't help in the role that you are applying for, think twice about whether another bullet point would be more relevant.
    b. Also, it helps you manage that one-page goal.
5. Use the job posting as a checklist: at least 80 percent of the qualifications and requirements on the posting should be covered by at least one (if not more) activities, and ideally accomplishments, described on your resume.
    a. The company has requirements for a reason; they want to make sure you can do the job. If you have done it, or better yet, have an achievement that proves that you've done it well, they can validate that you can do the role.
    b. More importantly, recruiters may not know anything about the job. Often the only information they have are the qualifications and requirements provided by the hiring manager. So, if they don't see the correlation between the qualifications provided and your resume, they can't recognize that you're a fit for the position.
    c. This also means that each resume should be tailored to the job. No need to overhaul the entire document every time you apply for a job, but at least make some tweaks and adjustments so that the requirements and qualifications on the job posting are easily identifiable on your resume.
    d. If you aren't willing to put thirty to sixty minutes into the tweaks, do you really want the job?

Following the last recommendation means that you will have multiple versions of your resume. We recommend that you consolidate and accumulate the achievements and activities to make a "super resume," which we call your "career document." Here you can store the different versions of your resume that are more focused on execution, leadership, or more related to a specific industry. You can then pick and choose versions of text from your career document that will make creating your resume easier and faster.

The FIRM will help you with guidelines on your resume that focus on "first principles" and the "why" we ask you to do so. You don't have to follow them, nor will following all of them guarantee you a job. However, most recruiters we've sampled agree with the recommendations in principle, and it will be up to you to put them into practice.

The one aspect we do highly, highly encourage is including achievements versus activities in your career document, as it better defines your value and shows that you can understand and manage expectations. Most people know their activities, and what they are expected to do, but many do not know what their achievements might be because few have a solid understanding of what is expected of them. They therefore cannot articulate that they did a good job. Clear expectations make it easier for everyone involved, and best of all, by understanding expectations, you now know what you need to do to be considered successful.

NOTE: if you follow the networking and BMC guidance and get a referral, you might be able to skip much of the resume inconvenience, since often even getting selected for an interview without a referral would be akin to winning the lottery.

David Maister's trust equation

Trust is important when servicing others. I was notified of the "trust equation" by a friend of mine, which originally came from David Maister, Charles H. Green, and Robert M. Galford and their book *The Trusted Advisor*. The trust equation is

$$\text{Trustworthiness} = \frac{\text{Credibility} + \text{Reliability} + \text{Intimacy}}{\text{Self-Orientation}}$$

Figure 10: Trust equation

In other words, someone trusts you if they believe:

- you *can* do it (you're credible)
- you *will* do it (you're reliable)
- you make them feel *secure* (you have intimacy with them)
- you have *their interests* in mind (you're *not* all about yourself)

That doesn't mean that you must be at the highest levels of the first three and the lowest of the last. It means that if you are deficient in one, you may need to overcompensate with another to build and maintain trust. Trust takes effort to build as credibility, reliability, and intimacy often develop over multiple interactions. If someone gets something done for you once, you will likely assume they can do the same thing again. But you might not be as willing to trust them the second time, having only one interaction as a frame of reference, as you would the eleventh time.

Building trust seems like common sense; however, some people are focused more on short-term gain and end up losing trust as a consequence. They then need to spend more effort than they would have in the first place to rebuild trust. In school, the stakes might seem to be smaller, so you might feel you can get away with it, but beware that it becomes a slippery slope. You may end up losing more trust than you intended.

TRY THIS: Reflect on and practice trust

Reflect on your most trusting and least trusting relationships. How can you improve trust in your relationships?

Chapter 10: The New Networking

Porter Gale's book *Your Network Is Your Net Worth* is very useful in helping to understand the importance of relationships. Networking often isn't done at all, or it's not done well. I offer Build Meaningful Connections (BMC) as an alternative to traditional networking. Networking tends to spawn visions of slimy salespeople shaking hands, handing out business cards, and engaging in superficial small talk. BMC looks to connect people and encourages you to be curious about others. It asks you to add value to others without expecting anything in return and suggests you stay connected and shape longer-term relationships.

School is a prime place to build relationships. You frequently interact with the same people. They are close proximity-wise, which means they are more readily available and valuable to you. Building on those relationships in the future could pay you back in multiples, especially if you don't expect any future returns.

Introverts can network, too

School, specifically university, was a bit of an awkward time for me. I did not know many people there. I was an introvert, but I wanted to be outgoing and meet lots of people. I managed to make a few friends and even found a girlfriend. But to deal with my emotions when that relationship ended, I focused on academics to avoid failing my courses. I previously shared my study-cube/carrel story and have since realized that my self-imposed label of "introvert" was part of what was holding me back. I have since realized that an introvert is not someone who wants to be alone, but someone who gets energized from spending time with small groups of people. Contrast that with an extrovert, who is invigorated in a large group. I learned that I could be an excellent networker even as an introvert, as long as I kept the circle of conversation small.

TRY THIS: Break the ice

Practicing your networking conversations can seem like you're forcing yourself to be something you're not. I disagree. You must find ways to make networking work for you. If you have no friends and have never made a Meaningful Connection with anyone, then what better reason to start? Give it a shot, and if you firmly feel that friends aren't right for you, you can always go back there. For everyone else, start practicing small and take every opportunity to practice. The first step to Building a Meaningful Connection is just to start the conversation. Here are some ways to practice starting the connection:

1. Ask questions that you already know the answer to.
    a. If you take transit, ask someone how long it will take to get to X station. Then extend the conversation by asking whether they've been to your stop or where their stop is.
    b. While waiting in line to get food at the cafeteria or food court, ask someone in front or behind you, "Have you had the X before?" If the answer is "Yes" then ask, "How was it?" If it's a "No" then ask, "Have you heard if it's good or not?"
    c. In the lunch room, whether you bring your lunch or not, try to spark a conversation. It is good to mix it up. Eating in a campus cafeteria allows you to connect with those who do not go out. Talk about what you've all brought to eat. Conversations about food tend to be natural in a lunch room. Then practice easing into another topic. Not bringing your lunch allows you to find those who also need to buy food. Talk about the place you're eating at, or ask for a recommendation for other places they've frequented.
2. Be observant: Sherlock Holmes had a knack sizing up people through the clothing they wore and what they carried with them. Try to do the same to initiate a conversation.
    a. Look at what they are holding. Are there any logos on their bag or jacket? You might be able to say, "Ah, you also go to XYZ collegiate? My cousin went there."
    b. Compliment them on their choice of clothing: "That's a nice hat. Where did you get it?"
    c. Point out items of interest: "That's a very interesting watch. Could I ask you more about it?"

3. Be curious:
   a. A conversation can be like a tennis match. You serve up a question and put the conversational ball into the other person's court. You hope they answer the question, sending the ball back to you so you can return it again. While this worked for a while and helped me practice, I found my connections were not very meaningful.
   b. Asking questions instead to find information about the person, their SIWIKE, or just to have an interesting experience, made for a more meaningful conversation. Finding more about their hometown, how their aunt influenced them in their career decision, how their experience at X was. The detective work to find those interesting tidbits can be quite fun, and you never know what you'll learn in the process.
4. Set practice goals: goals help with focus so practice doesn't seem as random.
   a. Start with one a week, and try to get to one a day. (You can reduce this as you get the hang of initiating and maintaining more meaningful conversations.)
5. Reflect and learn.
   a. As you hit your connection goals, you don't want to just start random conversations for the sake of it. You want to reflect and learn how to make them better and more meaningful for you and the person you are connecting with.
6. Forced engagement.
   a. Some people will find practicing easy, but for those who need help, forced engagement might be the right way to go. Try putting yourself in situations where you are required to initiate interactions or where others need to initiate interactions with you. Groups like Toastmasters, doing improv, or even salsa dancing are events where others will be around to engage with you.

At this point, your goal is not to necessarily make a connection meaningful, but to just make the connection. Then you can attempt to steer the conversations to be more meaningful. And if you can do that with random strangers, you will be much more likely to be able to do this with people who could influence your career.

The best part of these seemingly random connections is that you never know when serendipity will hit. That seemingly random connection could end up unveiling a future opportunity. Or, at the very least, you helped to make someone's day a little less mundane.

Networking does not have to be sleazy — Build Meaningful Connections

Do you network like a credit card or a debit card? Most people approach networking as a credit card. They ask people for their time over coffee or lunch or drinks and start taking. Taking their time. They accumulate a little debt. They ask them to review their resume. A little more debt. They ask them to connect them to someone. More debt. When will that debt ever be repaid? What if you approached the relationship by giving first? Be authentically curious about the person you are trying to connect with, and allow them to tell their story and speak about their favourite subject, themselves! You just made a small deposit. You can connect them to someone who could help them with something they mentioned. Another deposit. Suggest a resource you can share. Another small deposit. You recommend a Thai restaurant because they just told you they like Thai food. Another small deposit.

Professional connections are akin to personal connections. Consider your friend who's always giving and is generous with their time and their stuff. Then consider the friend who only calls when they need something. Which one do you want to be?

BMC is a long-term approach and is not about networking for the job right now. It's about building the relationship for the job you might have in three years or thirteen years or thirty-three years.

TRY THIS: Practice adding value

In a conversation, think about how you could help and add value. During every statement that the other person makes, ask yourself, "How could I help them with that?" and offer to help if it makes sense to you.

Networking is not a crapshoot

Now that you've practiced initiating conversations and turning them into meaningful exchanges, you want to start meeting people who might be important and meaningful to your career. I recommend setting goals, starting with making one connection per week and moving up to several per day. You can start with

1. Alumni: Whether you've graduated or not, your school is a great connection point. You can share experiences of similar classes or similar places on campus. If you've graduated, reaching out to those in your graduating class can expose you to experiences that others with your background have had. But remember, reaching out to alumni does not have to be limited to your program, faculty and others in the school.

2. Family and friends: Close relations are often overlooked as some people want to separate business from personal. However, by ignoring them you might be missing out on a great resource. Asking if others know anyone who works in your ideal role can be quite interesting; you never know which of your aunts does something very similar to your career goal, or your friend's older cousin could share their experiences of something you've always wanted to pursue, or your little sister's best friend's dad might be currently doing the job you want to have in ten years.

3. Current and previous co-workers: Most people are reasonably good at connecting with their current co-workers. This BMC network is focused on those in your company you don't interact with on a daily basis — the people in the company outside of your department with interesting histories, paths, and connections. When co-workers move to another company, it's important to stay in contact with them, as you never know what doors might open there. At the very least, you will continue to learn about what someone who sat next to you for the past few years is now doing and how they are applying their skillset to their new position. Also, when you move to another company, make sure to stay connected to as many people as you can in the previous company, as they might stay and continue their path, or they might also go elsewhere and open your eyes to new potential.

4. Market: Other people you've interacted with at conferences and events might have gone to a different school, but they might share a common background. Even though your skillsets and job titles might be very different, you often share similarities. You might also meet others in your market at volunteer organizations, extracurricular activities, and social groups. The members of your market network are often the most varied of your networks and another important source of opportunities.

5. Mentees: This one might seem out of place, but it is here because I believe that we would all benefit from sharing our own knowledge and experiences, our own SIWIKE, with others out there. I know for me, when I mentor someone and they come back to tell me that I made an impact, it's one of the greatest feelings. The flip side is that mentees are plugged into a different network of people and a broad network is always helpful. Learning more about them could potentially uncover opportunities you didn't know you had. Another interesting consideration is that a student sometimes surpasses their teacher, so don't be surprised if a mentee eventually becomes your peer or someone more senior than you. That potential future mentor would hopefully be more than willing to share their learning and insights with you!

Try turning connecting with people in your circle into an activity. Think of at least three people to place in each circle. Write down where they work and what they do. If you don't know, then that's a great person to reach out to. Start with those closest to you and work outwards. Make it a goal to connect with at least person per week. If you are on the job hunt, try to meet with at least one person per day!

Network Circles – Brainstorm

Circle	Who can I reach out to?	Where do they work? What do they do?
Family	1. 2. 3.	
Friends	1. 2. 3.	
Alumni	1. 2. 3.	
Work	1. 2. 3.	
Market	1. 2. 3.	
Mentors	1. 2. 3.	
Mentees	1. 2. 3.	

Figure 11: Network brainstorm

People often ask me how big their network should be. My typical response is, as big as you can manage. Then there's the inevitable question of quantity versus quality. And my typical response is both. Ideally, you should network with everyone you can (sometimes the lower-level folks are more influential than you can imagine). A few will reciprocate. Those are the ones you will keep furthering your BMC relationship. Your network "tree" will grow and naturally prune itself. And it's always nice to occasionally see a dying branch and help it grow again. To answer the question, a general rule would be to go by Dunbar's number of 150. The psychologist Robin Dunbar did research on people's networks, and his statistical analysis found that 150 is the limit of how many people one person can connect with and have a stable relationship with. The number actually ranges from 100 to 250, but most people agree that 150 is a good average. If you are in that ballpark, your network is healthy, and you can choose whether you want to be on the higher or lower end.

The tactical goal could be to meet at least one new person a week. Just the title of Keith Ferrazzi's book, *Never Eat Alone*, could give you a much loftier goal. He doesn't mean that you need to eat lunch with a different person every day (repeats are allowed), but it's great if you can manage it. At one point, I'd have breakfast with one person, morning coffee with another, lunch with someone else, afternoon coffee with another person, then after work drinks and possibly a late coffee or drinks after dinner with other people. And all this was scheduled around my full-time job.

You can also network using your resume. How would you do that? For each company or organization that you list on your resume, add at least three (more if possible) people that you've interacted with. For school, take a look at your graduating class, as well as alumni from different years. For volunteer and extracurricular groups, consider fellow volunteers as well as supervisors and leaders. For work, consider reports, peers and leaders, irrespective of if they are still at the company or not. Then cross out everyone you've interacted with in the last six months. The ones remaining are the ones you need to reach out to and catch up with.

Another interesting technique when you're meeting someone you meet with regularly for a catch up is to bring a friend and ask them to do the same. That can be another great way for people to meet and help expand each other's networks.

TRY THIS: Assess your network health

Map out your network health against the various network circles. Work on building your network where it is light.

It pays to be the dumbest person in the room

Playing up is about surrounding yourself with those who are better than you in your areas to improve. You've probably had that experience where you're among the best at what you do. You feel empowered when playing. And you've probably had the opposite experience, when you're the worst player and feel a little embarrassed that you're dragging down the team. In the first "playing down" scenario, you might feel good, but it is a much more challenging situation to learn and get better, as getting better often involves challenging yourself and improving in difficult circumstances. In the second "playing up" scenario, you surround yourself with better players, and everyone is a mentor for you, so it's much easier to watch, learn, and improve. If you have the opportunity and want to improve, play up instead of down. Although, sometimes it's just about hanging around with friends, which is fine in either case.

Taking the concept to the top level, if you can learn from the best in your chosen field and surround yourself with those world-class people in your field to have them help you be the best version of you, you can really boost your career potential.

Within my group of friends, I was pretty good at sports. In volleyball, I definitely wasn't great, but better than average. However, as my group of friends diversified, more and more of them were in the "good at volleyball" camp versus the "I was better at volleyball than they were" camp. The trouble was, I wanted to play in the "I was better at volleyball than they were" camp. I'd play. Move around. But never really got any better. When folks from the first camp called to ask me to play, I wouldn't be available. I'd be too tired or want to get a snack or some other excuse. I didn't realize what I was doing until after I read Carol Dweck's book *Mindset*. When the folks who weren't as good were on the court, I'd be the first one ready to play. But when the "hardcore" folks played, I just wanted to sit in the shade. I had many opportunities to "play up" and potentially get better, but I was stopping myself from capitalizing on those opportunities and learning from those better players because of my ego.

TRY THIS: Assess your place in the room

Reflect on various situations throughout the week. Assess whether you were the smartest or dumbest, or most-skilled or least-skilled person in the room, or somewhere in between. In areas where you are closer to the best, how could you become closer to the worst (i.e., how could you surround yourself with smarter people)?

Future opportunities come from past connections

Most people make an effort to connect for the "now." Meeting someone in the hopes of getting a job "now." Hoping they can do you a favour and connect with someone "now." However, the best thing to do is to start the connection "now," when you don't need anything, and build it into a Meaningful Connection, not with the hopes that you can cash in on it, but with the hopes that if you ever needed to, you could. That may mean reconnecting in five months, several times over five years, or even longer to help keep the connection warm and open. However, it is often hard to remember to stay connected (I sometimes forget my kids' birthdays). So what can you do?

The simple solution is to put a reminder on your calendar. We don't have infinite memories, so a push in the right direction is welcome. Then, based on the reciprocated conversation, set another reminder. Set it sooner if the connection is stronger — one to three months — and later if the connection isn't as strong — up to nine months. Try not to go more than a year without reconnecting, as it's very challenging to have any sort of Meaningful Connection without some sort of frequency. If you do this, you will have lots of reminders in your calendar. But let's say you message someone in February, and feel you should follow up with them in five months; you can add them to the reminder in your calendar already set for July. The benefit is that you have that time blocked off on your calendar, so it will help you remember. If your memory is better than mine, you might not need reminders. Or you can just agree that we're all human and set the reminders just in case.

The reminder notification is nothing without the actual follow-up message (I have snoozed the notification for a later time and sometimes dismissed it completely, potentially losing many opportunities as a result). So, make the time to send the messages. If I told you that reconnecting with that person in six months would mean that you'd get a $5,000 cheque, would you do it? Those interactions might very well lead to a similar gain in the future. You'll never know how much value you might be ignoring by not sending that message.

LinkedIn, Facebook, and other social media sites are also useful tools to remind you of work anniversaries, job changes, birthdays, and other reasons or reminders to reconnect. They have a history of your communication with the other person and allow you to include notes (which you need to be diligent about updating after in-person connections). Some people might feel that writing notes about a person is insincere, but for me, taking the time to record my ideas helps me to retain the information much more easily. And if I can bring up that information in our next meeting, the person I interacted with knows that I care enough to remember.

TRY THIS: Schedule your follow-ups

For each person you meet in the next month, set a calendar invite three to nine months from now, and make it recurring and without an end date. Batch them by quarter or term or bi-monthly. Or pick a time scale that feels comfortable to you. For any past connections that you feel are relevant, add them to your reminders. Make sure you make contact when the appointment appears.

Chapter 11: Summary — Skill Building

1. Turn excuses to purpose.
2. Become better at setting expectations.
3. Build good habits.
4. Experiment with time management and prioritization.
5. Reframe selling for you.
6. Be a better customer server.
7. Find your role.
8. Update your resume.
9. Practice interviewing.
10. Map out interview seasons.
11. Get experience.
12. Track your job hunt.
13. Practice managing.
14. Build your job hunt essentials.
15. Practice Building Meaningful Connections and adding value.
16. Assess and maintain your network health.

The most important guidance I have for building your skills is to start now and continue building them. Don't wait until you're about to graduate. If you only focus on your grades, when it gets close to graduation and you finally start writing your resume, you'll find it to be pretty sparse, with only a degree and no experiences to write down. It all comes down to practice. Interviewing is a skill. Networking is a skill. With practice you can get better at them both. Make an effort to practice, and make practice a priority.

Skill building: Resources

Peter Drucker

A titan when it comes to management and leadership groups. Many of his books, such as *The Effective Executive*, are classics in the business world and are a goldmine of timeless information.

Books: *The Effective Executive*

This book was quite useful to reinforce many of the things I had learned about leadership as well as provide new insights.

Career tests and assessments

Career tests such as Sokanu (http://sokanu.com), O-Net Online (http://onetonline.org), and similar resources help people recognize their talent related to potential career paths. They are good resources for those who don't know what they want to do or where their talents lie. But don't just follow the results blindly. Include them as another data point as part of your self-analysis process.

Career tools and management tools

A great podcast and collection of business perspectives. I relate to a lot of what they say, and they offer quite a lot of tactical advice focused on jobs, people, and work management.

Podcasts

http://www.manager-tools.com/podcasts/career-tools

The podcast is bundled with manager tools, which are still relevant for anyone looking to learn more about the working world. Some of the suggestions are quite directive and prescriptive with little flexibility, but I appreciate why they've provided such clear-cut guidance; it's so that only those that really understand the implications of doing something different would deviate from their directions. Overall, it is a great resource for someone wanting to make the most of the working world.

Books

I've read these books and I definitely recommend reading them to further empower you in your career. Most are recent publications, and I have already discussed many of their points in this book; however, the books go into much more detail than I had the space for.

Your Network Is Your Net Worth by Porter Gale: provides many insights on the power of relationships for work.

What Got You Here Won't Get You There by Marshall Goldsmith: Marshall is a renowned career coach and hearing his insights would be helpful for any budding executive.

Just Listen by Mark Goulston: a good book on the topic of communication.

Getting Things Done by David Allen: considered to be one of the bibles of productivity, David Allen systematizes task execution in his GTD system. While I don't implement GTD to the letter, I have found some parts useful to incorporate into my productivity practices.

The Power of Habit by Charles Duhigg: In an earlier section I have an image, Figure 6, that I say I adapted from the book. While the image itself didn't really come out of the book, creating it was heavily influenced by the book's content. I thought it was a good way to represent the process of changing a habit.

Procrastinate on Purpose by Rory Vaden: his concept of Significance was so enlightening that I incorporated it into the classic Eisenhower Matrix graphic.

Part 4: Expansion

Chapter 12: Lifelong Learning

You're set up for success. But the journey doesn't stop when you graduate. It's actually just beginning. You'll want to keep a few more things in mind to be truly successful as you enter the working world.

Your first job is not forever

What I did not realize or appreciate during school was that my first job did not have to be permanent. It seems like common sense, but at the time, I thought that if I was a developer first, I would be a developer until I retired. Or maybe a senior developer or a managing developer or some other sort of developer. Now I understand that soft skills and even hard skills can be applied to multiple areas. My skills as a developer helped me to logically structure thoughts and ideas. Don't restrict yourself to just titles, industries, or companies.

Now that you understand the job hunt process, try to take the job that you want and reverse-engineer it through the process. Consider the previous conversation we had about roles in the "I can reverse-engineer my dream job" section and see how you stack up. A good way is to find alumni in jobs that you want and see how your experience stacks up to theirs. The gap builds you a nice little plan on what to work on in the next few months and years. Examining your experiences and seeing how they are relevant for the role is also important to get through the job hunt process.

TRY THIS: Brainstorm future versions of you

Brainstorm other paths that you can take. Explore other experiences. Use BMC to work with people in your areas of interest and curiosity.

The path to success is rarely straight or narrow

The SIWIKE I learned (and wish I did more of) in secondary and post-secondary school is to explore a diverse range of experiences. I should have spent more time learning things outside of computers and technology, things related to business, arts, and the humanities. I am happy with my decision, but a more diverse base of experiences would have helped me answer the question, "How do you know you don't like it if you haven't even tried it?" I am so impressed by many of the students I encounter. They can and do take advantage of all the opportunities in front of them. Equally, I am disappointed in those that don't take advantage of the opportunities that are provided to them.

If you think your North Star is related to a certain discipline, then find a club or organization that caters to that discipline. Participating in a business group, science club, humanities organization, competition, conference, or another event is a great way to start. Your school probably has a website of all the student clubs. Pick a few that are of interest, or start one if you see a gap! There are also other organizations not associated with schools often run by the government, local communities, or just started by someone who saw a need and wanted to bring like-minded people together. Gaining more exposure and starting to build a network will be well worth the time you put in now, and it might pay off in the future.

Also, consider exposing yourself to interests outside of what you might normally consider your general career direction. Let's say you're headed towards pursuing a degree in business; perhaps trying your hand at coding might be worth a shot if coding interests you. Maybe teaching interests you; in that case, you can leverage programs available to teach younger students about money. Often finding your passion involves trying things out. You try something and find out you are interested, maybe not in everything you are doing, but in some of it. You might then find another opportunity that better fits that thing you found interesting. And you get better at it, and do more of it, and eventually realize that you might have found a passion. But not until you first try!

Having a variety of experiences where you can find opportunities and explore is important in finding what you are inspired to do. There are so many things that you could do in this world, and you're only exposed to a fraction of them up until the time you finish school. Leverage your time during your school years and use it to explore, and after your school years you can find what your inspiration is.

Here are some guidelines:

- First year — join as many clubs as you can manage. Likely the most that you could do is five over a term (approximately one per school day). Any more and you're probably spreading yourself too thin.

- Second year and onwards — pick one to two clubs that you want to focus on, one you feel will continue to help you grow or that you enjoy and gives you a sense of fulfillment. Add one or two more as part of your "20 percent time." Consider becoming an executive member of one of the clubs.

TRY THIS: Try one new activity each month

Take interesting electives. Join clubs. Do volunteer work. Things related to your degree. Things unrelated to your degree. Explore. Build Meaningful Connections throughout your diverse experiences. Try one new interest every term.

Add to and adjust your career bucket list

Conventional wisdom is that you go to school, get a job, then retire. Starting work at twenty to twenty-five, retiring between sixty and sixty-five, that's about forty work years. And the job you got was often "for life," with twenty-, thirty-, or forty-year careers being common. Many companies have service award programs that celebrate those milestones. In today's world, the lifelong job is more the exception than the rule. Further to that, people today often pivot, changing jobs over the course of their work life multiple times to roles that may be totally different or only partially related to the previous one. A pivot in the start-up world is a change in direction. Facebook started as Facemash where you would see pictures of two people and were asked to rate which was hotter. They pivoted and are now, well, Facebook. Apple originally provided kits so that hobbyists could build their own computers. They pivoted by fully assembling them.

In the career sense, your pivot could be starting in accounting, then moving into technology or vice versa. Or starting as a developer, then moving into management consulting, then pivoting again to become a career coach. That wasn't your grandparents' career, but these career pivots are becoming more and more frequent. Why? I am not exactly sure, though I am sure it has something to do with the instant nature of today's society. In grandpa's day, you had to apprentice for twenty years before getting into a role. Now you could probably ask Siri,

Google it, or find it on YouTube and figure it out to become proficient in years, months, weeks, or even hours.

That points to another challenge. If the traditional path was to do one thing, what about people who want to do many things? Some even want to do everything. With just a limited choice, it's no wonder so many students become paralyzed with what to do for their careers. Our suggestion is not to choose, but instead create your *career bucket list*. For anyone who doesn't know, a "bucket list" is a list of things you want to do before you die, like visiting the Pyramids and the Great Wall of China or go skydiving. When applied to your career, it's more along the lines of wanting to be a manager, a senior executive, starting your own business, or working abroad. With a career bucket list, it's not about doing that one thing for life. It's about achieving what you want in life.

I also suggest you assess your career bucket list every year or so:

1. You can check in to see if you're making progress towards one or more of your goals.
2. Consider if they are still relevant based on your current life circumstances (perhaps add, remove, or reorder the items based on priorities).

My own journey took me from the technical side, as a programmer and developer, to the business side towards process engineering, across supply chain processes, and ultimately towards career coaching and advising.

On the spectrum of career changes, there are people who know what they want to do and focus their entire careers on their choice. If you have that direction, that's great. If you don't have that focus and want to have a broader variety of professions, that's fine as well, but don't neglect those items on your career bucket list. Pick one to focus on, and start crossing them off!

When you are searching for jobs, most people have a narrow view of their "job shopping list," what they can do, and what's important to them. They don't focus on roles or companies outside the stereotypical ones associated with their degrees. But sometimes you are equipped with transferrable skillsets, which might qualify you for jobs only tangentially related to your degree. Here are some examples:

- A Bachelor of Commerce graduate who excelled at connecting with people found themselves well suited to a role in sales.

- A chemical engineer was always interested in food and took their process view to food services to find ways to improve the preparation of food while maintaining a high level of quality.

- A psychology major took their understanding of human behaviours and applied it to marketing.

For many that I've coached, it's often a matter of opening their thinking to the job possibilities in the marketplace. When you are focused on your books and courses, thinking outside of what you know is hard. Challenging yourself by building relationships and making meaningful connections with people is a great way to consider not only what is possible but also what has already been done. For example, if you found alumni who graduated five to ten years ahead of you, you are likely to find people on very different career paths along with the ones in the traditional roles that you considered. Since they were in your program, they could provide you with step-by-step directions to get there if that destination is interesting to you. It is ultimately your decision on whether you follow all, most, or none of those steps.

In any case, it is often useful to challenge your own assumptions and be open to other opportunities out there.

Some of the people I mentor are stressed out about finding the perfect job. They only apply to a select few roles because those are the roles that they want to do. That can be paralyzing, especially if they are not focused on BMC to extend their reach. They are worried about making the decision between a "okay" job versus searching for the dream job they might never get. Although each decision is unique, an important consideration is whether you could take that "okay" job and make the very best version of that job possible. Could you leverage your time there to connect with more professionals to help you get closer to the roles you truly want? Could you coach yourself to make each day the best *ever*? Could you acquire a new achievement that would make a great new bullet point on your resume? You should take every opportunity to make it just that, an opportunity for you to continue your journey towards your career potential.

Being heads down at school, we are often so focused on graduation and the end goal of getting a job that we forget that there is a lot more time afterwards. Most people don't have the same car for their entire lifetime, nor live in the same house. So why would a career, let alone a job, be any different? It's not like you are marrying your job or your employer. You should always be open to opportunities and make the switch if the opportunity is right. Or use it to validate how amazing your current opportunity is. Opportunities could also be with the same employer. You might be a lifer at a company but move from customer-facing service roles to back-office management to sales to advisory to an executive role.

Many students have an expectation of a perfect job right out of school. Often, the reality is that you might have to go through multiple jobs to get to where you want to be. Based on the pace of change of the world, it is more likely that jobs will become shorter and shorter in duration, not necessarily because you want to do something different, but perhaps because some jobs will cease to exist and new jobs will take their place. If you're lucky to find a job that you spend your entire career doing, that's great if you're happy, it excites you, and it gives you fulfillment. If not, that's fine too. There are plenty of opportunities out there for those who want them!

TRY THIS: Create your career bucket list

Create your career bucket list. Set a calendar reminder to review it annually.

Find your inner critic

It is quite interesting how we are not taught *how* to learn. In school we learn through formulated classes and structures. However, just as we're varied as people, we are also varied in how we learn. There are theories that some people learn better through sight, sound, or touch (kinesthetic). Finding out how you learn best is important. We might also learn different things better in some ways than in others. For instance, some people are better conceptual learners, and they start understanding general concepts before internalizing the application (deductive thinking), while others grasp ideas through examples and then extend them to broader situations (inductive thinking).

Additionally, critical thinking is an important skill when learning to learn. Critical thinking seems straightforward, but too many people go through life without ever considering whether their decisions are appropriate or what the implications of these decisions are. Assumptions are taken as facts. Directions are not validated with appropriate rationale. You do exactly as you are told. That doesn't mean that you must question every little thing, but it does mean that you want to be mindfully aware and to test assumptions on the "correctness" of what you are doing. If it's working, it's probably correct. If it's not working, you might want to try something else. And be aware that just because it has worked in the past does not necessarily mean it will continue to work. That's why I often get people to spend time reflecting on what's working, what's not, and how they could improve.

The typical critical thinking framework uses the W5H questions (who, what, why, when, where, and how) to assess the various contexts of what you're learning. Another way to think critically is to understand the context of when it is applicable. I'm sure you've heard this classic parental question: "If Jimmy jumped off a bridge, would you jump too?" Just because it is right for Jimmy does not mean it will be right for you. If Jimmy was a spy running from a squad of assassins, maybe jumping off the bridge would be a good idea, but wouldn't be for you as an innocent bystander. But if there was a pride of hungry looking lions on the bridge with nowhere else to run, maybe jumping with Jimmy isn't such a bad idea. Silly examples aside, approaching problems with a bit of critical thinking can help, especially with unfounded assumptions.

School provides a lot of teaching, but doesn't always teach you to think critically, which is quite often the key foundational way of adding value in creative and analytical work. You can get through life quite easily just by being able to follow directions, and thinking critically will help add even more value. While school often teaches you to provide a standard answer, real-life problems do not always have a single perfect or universal answer. It is often more important to ask the right question than simply answer the question asked of you. And if you can intentionally take another person or group's point of view, you will likely learn the material more thoroughly.

Memory is also an important aspect of learning. Socrates said, "There is no learning without remembering," and it's quite amazing — considering the Greeks and other classical civilizations used a multitude of techniques to train your memory — that memory-improving techniques are not taught in schools. Most people feel they were either born with a good memory or not. Concepts like genetic memory, where some people were born with abilities, point to nature having a role, but lots of research points to the ability to nurture memory in order to improve it. And while I am by no means a memory champion, I can attest to the fact that my memory has improved with practice and training, though it could always be improved further.

TRY THIS: Practice critical thinking

Reflect on times in the past month where you could have uncovered something earlier had you thought about it critically. Program yourself to be aware of future situations.

Knowledge shared is knowledge multiplied

The SIWIKE of being a mentor might seem out of place in this section, but you need to understand that as you get further in your career, the more you'll be on the receiving end of people wanting to connect with you. So, the goal would be to pay back some of the generosity that others provided to you by providing your own SIWIKE to future generations. If you have five to ten mentors, you should also have five to ten mentees. Many of your mentees may have their own networks and connections that could be of help to you.

People ask me how many mentors I have, and I usually tell them hundreds, even thousands. This is because I treat everyone as a potential mentor in that I know I could learn something from everyone. I just have to be curious enough to find out what that is (and you should be too). Maybe you don't categorize someone you get guidance from one time as a mentor, but intending to find out what you can learn from others is relevant to being a good mentee and to being a mentor to others.

I also expand my definition of mentors to the authors of the books I read, the producers of the podcasts I listen to, and the creators of any content that I consume that helps me learn. Reading has been a fantastic way for me to get access to mentors that I might not ever meet. I have a lot of mentors that I have never met. I hope to one day reach out to them and thank them for helping shape my career and life.

When you do the network brainstorm exercise (Figure 11), don't forget to find a few mentees as well.

TRY THIS: Help someone else improve

Find someone you can mentor. Share your SIWIKE.

You've got more time than you think

I started out my entrepreneurial journey at thirty-six. The entrepreneurial world is not just for the twenty-somethings. This might seem way beyond your years, and I'll get to the point shortly.

If you have had several jobs since graduation, it's not too late to let your entrepreneurial tendencies take over and to start your own endeavours. You don't have to quit your job and take on unnecessary risks. You can do your normal job and explore your passion project after dinner or after the kids (you might eventually have) go to bed. That extra weekday evening time from 7 p.m. to 12 a.m. is basically a full work day given that most jobs have meetings and other time-sucking activities that mean most people work productively for about five hours per day. Don't have that much time? Spend whatever time you can manage. Keep in mind that the time you spend does compound and you'll get out the effort that you put in. Plus, if you're truly passionate about it, it won't even feel like work. It's just a fun hobby you're doing on the side, and occasionally you're getting paid for it.

Besides, unlike the movie *The Matrix*, you could always plug yourself back into the machine and work as an employee again. That should mitigate most of your fears about risk. Yes, you won't necessarily be as far ahead as you were, but you can have all sorts of other great experiences and perhaps cross off something on your career bucket list in the process.

You're not even close to forty, so how does all of this talk relate to you? I've spoken to a bunch of people who seemed to think they missed the boat because they didn't hit their targets by sixteen, twenty, thirty, or whatever age they were aiming for. I know that I've missed a bunch of my targets. But just because you might have as well doesn't mean you should give up. You have plenty of runway left to take off and make a difference to yourself, to those around you, and to the world. It isn't too late.

Having a mortgage and 1.5 kids (the second was on its way) made my decision to be self-employed quite challenging. I first took a contract role (which paid a bit more and had relatively lower time commitments), and I used the extra time to start building the business. When the contract ended, I used extra funds as my "seed funding" to allow me to go full-time. If things had gone south at any point, I would have still had diverse experience and my network; I could have always gotten a job somewhere. So, while you might have to take a chance and work hard while living off instant noodles for a little longer, or even move back in with your parents, you still have a lot time to turn yourself into a success. Taking calculated risks while you're young is much easier than when you're older. So if you're thinking about doing it, get to it sooner rather than later.

TRY THIS: Start something new

Follow your curiosity and interests and start something new this year.

All my dreams can come true — but not all at once

Today's society is filled with instant gratification. You can have a meal in seconds. You can learn about pretty much anything you want by asking the concierge on your phone. You can have whatever you want delivered to you in hours (by flying drones or otherwise). We hardly need to wait for anything. That makes patience a challenging virtue to have. In the working world, however, patience does pay off. Remember compound interest? If you start saving early, over the years the money grows at an exponential rate. If you withdraw that money early, you don't enjoy the same growth in wealth. So invest early. Perhaps you should start at the ground floor of a business and hustle to learn it inside and out. Learn all the intricacies and interrelations that work together to compound value for each other. Learn how a more effective HR department hires better people for sales, which provides more money for research and development, which allows for more innovative offerings for the marketing department, and so on. Eventually, you will know of all the places where value can exist in that business. Now all you must do is extract it. But if you stop when you only know half of the business, the intricacies and subtleties are not so apparent and value is harder to come by.

Being patient isn't about sitting and waiting. It is about providing value so that what comes out compounds what you put in. A key part of patience means doing the work and gaining experience. Investing in yourself. Investing in others. Providing value to others.

A classic example of patience (or lack thereof) is networking. Too many people network to get a job. Going to an event. Handing business cards or resumes. Can you get me a job? No. Then move to the next. Too few people network to build relationships and demonstrate value so that the other person absolutely wants to hire you. Going to an event. Being interested in the person. Finding out where you can add value to that person. Adding the value to that person. Having that person realize that this person is amazing at adding value, so I should make them a job offer or otherwise figure out a way to continue to work with them. That's how it's done.

In my experience, there were many eager (typically young) hires who wanted a title higher up than their demonstrated ability. Some were promoted far too quickly and ended up in problematic situations. They demonstrated their ability to do the work and did an exceptional job, but only did it once: for one client, on one project. They didn't necessarily put in the work over the right amount of time and their impatience got the better of them. They were persistent and vocal and were promoted on the belief that they could do it. Many ended up burning out because they had not developed the skills to manage situations properly. They could have used a bit of patience to make sure that they truly understood the challenges ahead of them. On the flip side, I saw others in a similar situation who could have moved more quickly but decided to spend more time and focused attention adding value to others. They had many opportunities presented to them that turned out to be much more beneficial to them in the long run.

TRY THIS: Stop and smell the roses

Pause, take a day off, and do something unproductive. Focus on the longer term.

You can create your passion

You will read many articles and recommendations on following or finding your passion and pursuing what you love. Look for what gives you excitement and meaning at the same time. I suggest that you create your passion instead. Here is why: your passion needs to start with an interest. Something that peaks your curiosity. Most people have a lot of interests. When you start pursuing that interest and move your skill level towards mastery, mastery of that interest can become your passion. It is often the pain and struggle to reach mastery that turns the interest into a passion.

As an example, Tony Robbins's *Money: Master the Game* reminded me of a science-fiction TV show called *The Twilight Zone*. Every episode ended in a twist. In the episode I am thinking of, a man with a passion for gambling has made and lost a fortune at casinos. In the episode, he dies. He wakes up in a luxurious room greeted by a man in a white suit. He is shown a wardrobe of tailored suits and stylish shoes to wear. He is escorted to a blackjack table and instructed to start playing. His first hand is a winning hand! And again, blackjack! He plays another game and wins! Game after game he keeps winning! His chip stack is growing incredibly! With all his success, women around him take notice and he ends the evening on a winning note with one of them back in his hotel room. He wakes up invigorated with his luck and heads back down to play again. Blackjack! Again and again. Every time. Day after day. Week after week. Month after month. The man soon gets bored and frustrated with winning. The dealer says, "You win" and the gambler replies, "Of course! I always win! I'm sick of this! I win every time." He speaks to the head man in a white suit and unleashes his frustration saying, "I'm so bored I'm going out of my mind! You know what? There must be some mistake. I'm not that good a person. I'm in the wrong place. I don't deserve to be in heaven!" The man in white smiles and says, "What makes you think this is heaven…?"

When things come easy, it can be great, but sometimes it can be boring, like for the gambler in the story. Often the effort you put in, the challenge of growing and improving yourself, is the catalyst for a passion. It even becomes self-reinforcing. You love it because you spent time figuring out how to do it well, and the achievement is meaningful for you. Which makes you want to improve more, which makes it even more meaningful. And so on.

Just be aware that a passion can have a tipping point when it becomes all-consuming. You want to be cautious not to get to that point because many things start to become neglected. Keep that passion as something that inspires you every day, but be sure to maintain some balance.

TRY THIS: Follow your curiosity, invest in an interest, and create your passion

Reflect on what you are curious about. Schedule some time to explore that curiosity. Find the areas of curiosity and continue with what is most interesting. How could you make it more interesting? How could you add more value?

Chapter 13: Unstoppable

Live life in the front row

One of the phrases that changed my perspective was to "live life in the front row," which clicked when I heard about the Front Row Foundation started by Jon Vroman. When I was growing up, I was always wondering why someone would volunteer at a show to come up in front of the audience and do whatever it was the show called for. I'd rather sit back, watch them, and judge them as they are tricked by the magician or become the butt of a choreographed joke or look foolish as they not-so-elegantly do what the expert made look so easy. But then I wondered whether they were the foolish one for taking a risk and having an awesome experience, or if I was the foolish one for not taking the opportunity to have that experience. Another way to look at it is, if someone offered you the chance to meet the CEO, would you do it? If you have ambitions of climbing the corporate ladder, then sure. But even if you don't, why wouldn't you give it a shot and be curious and learn about someone who has been successful enough to get to the top spot of the company you work for? Even if you aren't interested in the company at all, wouldn't it be interesting to gain some knowledge and insight from someone who got to the top?

Living in the front row is not only about being as close to the stage as possible, it's about making the most out of every opportunity you have. Because if you do, perhaps the lead singer of the band that you spent a lot of money to see might grab you and pull you on stage. Or you might meet other super fans and connect over common areas of interest to develop a lifelong friendship. Or have some other opportunity to connect with greatness. The alternative is watching from afar, where all of that could happen as well, but at a much lower probability. So, live life in the front row. Why would you settle for the alternative?

TRY THIS: Say yes to any reasonable request

Be a yes person. Explore what might make you uncomfortable. Learn to be comfortable being uncomfortable. Find the best and most interesting thing about whatever unexpected thing you end up doing.

Mediocrity is the enemy

You have much more to offer the world than you give yourself credit for. I know this because I see this all the time with the people I mentor-coach. If you are comfortable, you aren't learning. Now, I don't want them to be totally anxious and sweating buckets, but I do want them out of their comfort zone and challenging themselves to do something different. Otherwise, they are stuck in a life of mediocrity. Yes, it can be tough when you've always played it relatively safe, and now you have settled down and have a spouse and kids and can't take too many risks. But the goal is not to put yourself in massive debt to "follow your dreams," it's to live a fulfilled life and get as close to your potential as possible.

Be aware of success, which does not necessarily mean being in the spotlight. And I'm saying be aware, not beware. Success is interesting and different for everyone. Your measures of success are different than mine, which are different than many others' views irrespective of whether they are close to you or not. Conventional wisdom measures success by money, fame, and status. At the end of the day, success is simply meeting or exceeding an expectation. If your expectation is to be number 1 and in the spotlight, being backstage supporting an amazing performance is not success. However, if success means enabling those around you to be the best they can, then it would be.

The main point of "success not necessarily being in the spotlight" is that you can absolutely reach your career potential by being the supporting actor or the number 2. You could even be the number 4 who supports those that support those who support those in the spotlight. Just be the best number 4 you can be, and make sure you're having a great time. Understand where you can make the most impact as your greatest achievement of success.

Another point is to avoid comparisons. We're all human and comparison is basically written into our DNA. It is tough to compare the contributions of an entrepreneur who started a million-dollar business with someone who made a modest income and was always contributing back to their community, helping hundreds to better their lives. Don't be afraid of doing something mediocre. Be aware when you're labelling something mediocre.

TRY THIS: Plan your today

Be constantly improving. Plan to constantly improve. Invest in improving yourself daily.

Seek mastery

Some people develop a career though tenure (just by doing it for a long time) and are okay to be good at what they do. I'd ask, "If you're spending all that time, why wouldn't you want to be great at what you do? Why not be one of the top five in the company, industry, city, province or state, country, or world?" In the "Do well in school" SIWIKE, the 10,000-hour rule is discussed. It applies here, as you're making deliberate progress to improve as you spend that time in your profession. Why not spend that time improving yourself to get to that next stage and seek mastery? I believe mastery is important in finding what you are inspired by as mastery gives you the confidence to know that you are making a difference and that your cause is relevant and important.

In a TED talk, Sal Khan, founder of Khan Academy, noted (and I'm paraphrasing) that in the middle ages there was a low literacy rate primarily because most people didn't feel that everyone had the innate capacity to be able to read. Nowadays in the developed world, not being able to read is the exception. We believe that almost everyone has the capacity to read. What assumptions are we making about the capacity of children and their ability to learn? Especially if it's because we haven't found an effective way to teach it? Could creativity be like reading? Artistic ability? Motivation? My hypothesis is that if we take a mastery-based approach to education, we wouldn't have students failing and dropping out. They would just be allowed to focus on where they were naturally disposed to add the most value.

What if all subjects were like that? We teach courses in an assembly-line fashion, pushing students forward by age versus ability. Khan used an analogy involving building a home that hit home for me. He says that the current education system is like building a home where the contractor sets the foundation and the inspector determines that the quality of the foundation gets a grade of 75 percent. The contractor continues building the next floor and the inspector comes back and determines that the quality of the wall construction gets a grade of 60 percent (it makes sense that it's lower than the foundation since the foundation wasn't solid in the first place). The contractor continues building the upper floor and the inspector comes back and says the quality gets a grade of 40 percent. Who would want to live in that house? And would we ever expect the quality of the upper floors to be better than the ground floor when they are not built on a solid foundation? If we worked until the foundation was strong before we continued building, it would be much more likely that the next floor would be solid and that subsequent floors would have a solid structure to build on.

Now apply that to the education system. When students are moved forward based on age, not mastery, can you blame a student without a solid foundation in grade five math to be doing poorly in math when they get to grades six, seven, eight, nine, and so on? Wouldn't you want the student to get a 90 or 100 percent in grade five math before they progress to grade six? Just like you'd want the quality of your home's foundation to be rated that high before they built the next floor.

The unfortunate part is that great teachers and educators are being blamed for a flawed system. It is amazing when teachers can get their students to improve, meaning that they had to make up for the insufficient learnings of previous years, plus get the student to the current standard.

If you went through the standard education system, you might have been subjected to a system that doesn't necessarily reflect your aptitude for the subject matter. Even though you might love something, if you grew up thinking you weren't good at it, that might have caused you to give up. You were not taught through a mastery approach that would have allowed you to capitalize on your natural talents. So, perhaps you should pick up that neglected interest again and learn it with an eye towards mastery to see if there might be more to it. Who knows, you might surprise yourself, and the world might be a better place because you did.

TRY THIS: Take school seriously

Improve your current school situation. Increase your marks. Take a strength and improve on it.

You can run your own company

We've already discussed entrepreneurship, but there are several words that are being added to the vocabulary surrounding owning your own business that you might *not* have heard, such as X-preneur (the X stands for a number of things). An intrapreneur is someone with entrepreneurial tendencies operating within a company, usually taking a grass-roots effort to implement change in a much larger, often slower-moving organization. I've also heard of a sidepreneur, someone who has a personal side project that earns them money, typically taking place after work hours are done. The definitions are as follows:

- An entrepreneur becomes successful when they find something that adds value to people, whether that's sharing information via a social media platform, providing a product that makes lives easier, or providing a service that saves time or entertains people. Without an evolution of that value, the success of the entrepreneur dwindles.

- An employee on the other hand is hired for a specific set of functions, and unfortunately many never go beyond what is listed in their job description. They don't evolve and their value is limited. An "intrapreneur" uses their entrepreneurial tendencies to deliver value to the parts of the organization they support whether that's a bullet point on their job description or not. Adding value to other parts of the organization makes you more successful in your job, which in turn makes the whole company successful. The intrapreneur will hopefully one day be rewarded for the value they provided.

- A sidepreneur is often looking to switch positions or do something they love while maintaining the safety net of their regular nine-to-five job. This is what I did for a while. It is a risk-mitigated way for you to keep on your current path while exploring opportunities on the side.

TRY THIS: Start something annually

Start something. Make the most out of your time. Find where you can add most value.

There's no time like the present

This title of a novel by Primo Levi (in Italian it's *Se non ora, quando?*) might sound like a cliché, but the words are quite interesting once you consider your purpose. Most people have a lot they want to accomplish, but they often push it until later. Later is fine, but you must make sure that later doesn't turn into never. This was an important realization in my journey, and there are two things you should know about it:

1. You will *not* have more energy than you do now.
    - It's often quoted as "you will never be any younger" or something of that nature. Most people agree that twenty-five is when you peak and start to plateau physically, so if you got this book early, you might still have a few more years. But I did most of my reflecting when I was older. And as I grow older, I find myself needing to warm up and stretch before sports and exercise much more than I used to. I also need more naps and other down time. So, to be able to accomplish as much as you want, it is better to start sooner rather than later.

2. You will never have less responsibility than you do now.
    - With a second kid on the way, I was thinking, *Not now*. But then I asked myself, *When?* When they are four and six and at school and starting all their extracurricular commitments? At twelve and fourteen as one is about to head into high school? At sixteen and eighteen when university is around the corner? At twenty-two or thirty-two or whenever they are starting a life more their own? By then I would be getting close to retirement, so maybe I should just wait until then? And then I think back to the previous point about whether my energy level will be the same.

So, the answer to "If not now, then when" can be "later." Just make sure that when later comes, it's not met by its less achievement-oriented cousin "later still."

TRY THIS: *Reflect on limiting beliefs*

Reflect on what you want to accomplish in the future. What can be done right now? Start it now and plan to finish it.

Chapter 14: Summary — Expansion

1. Brainstorm future versions of you.
2. Try something new.
3. Create your career bucket list.
4. Practice critical thinking.
5. Find mentors.
6. Mentor someone.
7. Exercise patience.
8. Follow curiosity and excitement.
9. Say yes.
10. Plan to be better.
11. Practice mastery.
12. Move the future up.

You are ready to make an impact. You have all the knowledge you need. The most important part will be to take that knowledge and turn it into action. Go out there and find your purpose! Make that impact you've always dreamed of. I know you can, and hopefully now you know you can too.

Chapter 15: Where Will Your Awesomeness Take You?

You've learned a whole bunch of new tools and techniques. Hopefully they have been very useful and you will put them into practice. Most importantly, I hope that you actually get there. Whatever your purpose is, make the effort to pursue your dreams and your goals.

I want to know about your progress. What in the book helped the most? What wasn't so helpful? Were you able to share these ideas or your own with others? Plus I'm curating more SIWIKE daily as I learn and grow from new experiences or reflect on previous ones. Feel free to contact me at **luki@focusinspired.com** and I'd love to hear from you!

Luki Danukarjanto is a computer scientist turned management consultant turned "unlocker of career potential." He helps people get unstuck, find their direction, and achieve results. He works with Toronto-based universities and colleges as well as with youths and young professionals around the city. He is an advocate for entrepreneurship and supports many start-up mentoring programs.

Luki wants to weave mentorship into the fabric of society, starting by making Toronto the mentorship capital of the world. He shares his SIWIKE: Stuff I Wish I Knew Earlier, which is essentially what a mentor shares. His focus is to "move the middle." The top ten to twenty percent will do fine without him. The bottom ten to twenty percent will be much more challenging to get to. It's the middle sixty to eighty percent that he wants to level up a notch or two. He's planned more books for different life stages. He's also working on an interactive app to share his ideas. His ultimate goal is to open up a school for soft skills and transform education.

Luki resides in Markham, just outside of Toronto, Canada, with his wife and two sons. If you're in the Toronto area, and even if you're not, he welcomes you to connect with him to see how he could be of help.

Commemoration

As a thank you for those that supported the crowdfunding campaign, I'd like to make special dedication to the following people who have been catalysts in the mission to weave mentorship into the fabric of society starting by making Toronto the mentorship capital of the world:

Val and Wies Danukarjanto

You've already given me so much and I appreciate your continued generosity. Thank you!

Jason Yeung

Your generosity literally brought tears to my eyes in knowing that a friend could be so generous. Thank you!

I appreciate your belief in me and in the mission.

FOCUS Inspired was founded by Luki to further his mission of weaving mentorship into the fabric of society, starting by making Toronto the mentorship capital of the world. FOCUS aims to transform education and help unlock career potential by sharing the Stuff I Wish I Knew Earlier. SIWIKE equips students with a curated toolkit of complementary educational resources on a foundation of self-awareness, choice, growth mindset, strengths, self-care and a thirst for personal improvement. Find out more at **http://focusinspired.com**.

www.ingramcontent.com/pod-product-compliance
Lightning Source LLC
Chambersburg PA
CBHW032226080426
42735CB00008B/732